MORE THAN **90** RECIPES FOR PASTA AND
NOODLE DISHES FROM AROUND THE WORLD

NOODLES

pil

Publications International, Ltd.

Pictured on the front cover: Mushroom Spaghetti *(page 72)*.

Pictured on the back cover *(counterclockwise from top left):* Three-Cheese Macaroni and Quinoa *(page 88)*, Chicken Ramen Noodle Bowls *(page 114)*, City Market Chicken Tarragon Penne *(page 14)* and Koshari *(page 182)*.

Photograph on front cover and pages 1 and 73 © Shutterstock.com.

ISBN: 978-1-64030-202-0

Manufactured in China.

8 7 6 5 4 3 2 1

TABLE OF CONTENTS

NOODLE SALADS

Fettuccine Niçoise Salad

Makes 4 servings

- 8 ounces green beans, cut into 2-inch pieces
- 1 package (9 ounces) uncooked fresh fettuccine
- ½ cup coarsely chopped pitted niçoise or kalamata olives
- 2 medium tomatoes, cored, seeded and chopped
- 1 can (6 ounces) tuna packed in water, drained and flaked
- ¼ cup olive oil
- 1 tablespoon white wine vinegar or fresh lemon juice
- ¼ teaspoon salt
- ¼ teaspoon black pepper
- ¼ cup finely chopped fresh basil

1. Bring large saucepan of salted water to a boil. Add green beans; cook 2 to 5 minutes or until bright green and crisp-tender. Transfer beans to colander with slotted spoon; drain well.

2. Return water to a boil. Add fettuccine; cook according to package directions. Drain and rinse under cold water until cool. Arrange fettuccine, green beans, olives, tomatoes and tuna on plates.

3. Whisk oil, vinegar, salt and pepper in small bowl; pour over salad. Sprinkle with basil.

Rotini, Chicken and Spinach Salad

Makes 4 servings

4 cups baby spinach

2 cups cooked rotini or elbow macaroni

1½ cups diced cooked chicken

1 tablespoon minced fresh chives

1 teaspoon minced fresh dill

3 tablespoons chicken broth

4 tablespoons olive oil

1 tablespoon lemon juice

1 teaspoon Dijon mustard

½ teaspoon salt

⅛ teaspoon black pepper

1. Combine spinach, pasta, chicken, chives and dill in large bowl; toss gently.

2. Whisk broth, oil, lemon juice, mustard, salt and pepper in small bowl. Pour over salad mixture; toss gently.

Thai-Style Warm Noodle Salad

Makes 4 servings

8 ounces uncooked angel hair pasta

½ cup chunky peanut butter

¼ cup soy sauce

¼ to ½ teaspoon red pepper flakes

2 green onions, thinly sliced

1 carrot, shredded

1. Cook pasta according to package directions.

2. Meanwhile, whisk peanut butter, soy sauce and red pepper flakes in serving bowl until smooth.

3. Drain pasta, reserving 5 tablespoons water. whisk hot pasta water into peanut butter mixture until smooth; toss pasta with sauce. Stir in green onions and carrot. Serve warm or at room temperature.

NOTES: This salad is as versatile as it is easy to make. It can be prepared a day ahead and served warm or cold—perfect for potlucks, picnics and even lunch boxes. You can also make it into a hearty meal by mixing in additional vegetables like julienned bell peppers or cooked broccoli, and leftover tofu, chicken or beef.

Chickpea Pasta Salad

Makes 4 servings

4 ounces uncooked spinach rotini or fusilli pasta

1 can (about 15 ounces) chickpeas, rinsed and drained

½ cup chopped red bell pepper

⅓ cup chopped celery

⅓ cup finely chopped carrot

2 green onions, chopped

3 tablespoons balsamic vinegar

2 tablespoons mayonnaise

2 teaspoons whole grain mustard

½ teaspoon salt

½ teaspoon black pepper

¼ teaspoon Italian seasoning

Leaf lettuce

1. Cook pasta according to package directions. Rinse under cold water until cool; drain well.

2. Combine pasta, chickpeas, bell pepper, celery, carrot and green onions in medium bowl.

3. Whisk vinegar, mayonnaise, mustard, salt, black pepper and Italian seasoning in small bowl until blended. Pour over salad; toss to coat. Cover and refrigerate up to 8 hours.

4. Arrange lettuce on individual plates; top with salad.

Country Time Macaroni Salad

Makes 4 servings

1   cup uncooked regular or whole wheat elbow macaroni

½   cup peas

½   cup chopped green bell pepper

⅓   cup thinly sliced celery

4   ounces ham, cubed

3   tablespoons mayonnaise

2   tablespoons plain yogurt or sour cream

2   teaspoons sweet pickle relish

¾   teaspoon dried dill weed

½   teaspoon yellow mustard

½   teaspoon salt

4   tablespoons (1 ounce) shredded Cheddar cheese

1. Cook pasta according to package directions. Rinse under cold water until cool; drain well. Place in medium bowl. Add peas, bell pepper, celery and ham.

2. Combine mayonnaise, yogurt, relish, dill weed, mustard and salt in small bowl; stir until well blended. Add to pasta mixture; mix well.

3. Stir in 2 tablespoons cheese. Sprinkle with remaining 2 tablespoons cheese. Serve immediately.

City Market Chicken Tarragon Penne

Makes 4 servings

4 ounces uncooked whole grain penne pasta

4 ounces fresh asparagus spears, trimmed and cut into 2-inch pieces

1½ cups diced cooked chicken

½ cup diced red onion

2 tablespoons canola oil

1 tablespoon lemon juice

1 tablespoon chopped fresh tarragon

1 tablespoon coarse grain Dijon mustard

½ teaspoon salt

¼ teaspoon black pepper

½ cup crumbled blue cheese

1. Cook pasta according to package directions. Stir in asparagus during last 3 minutes of cooking. Drain and place in large bowl. Add chicken and onion.

2. Meanwhile, whisk oil, lemon juice, tarragon, mustard, salt and pepper in small bowl. Add to pasta mixture; mix well.

3. Add cheese; stir gently.

TIP: This pasta dish is also good served cold. Sprinkle with fresh lemon juice just before serving.

Greek Pasta and Vegetable Salad

Makes 4 servings

1   cup uncooked corkscrew
     pasta or rotini

⅓   cup lime juice

2   tablespoons honey

1   tablespoon olive oil

1   clove garlic, minced

½   teaspoon salt

¼   teaspoon black pepper

4   cups fresh spinach

1   cup sliced cucumber

½   cup thinly sliced carrot

¼   cup sliced green onions

2   tablespoons crumbled feta
     cheese

2   tablespoons sliced pitted
     black olives

1. Cook pasta according to package directions. Rinse under cold water until cool; drain well.

2. Whisk lime juice, honey, oil, garlic, salt and pepper in large bowl. Stir in pasta. Cover; marinate in refrigerator 2 to 24 hours.

3. Combine spinach, cucumber, carrot, green onions, cheese and olives in large bowl. Add pasta mixture; toss to coat.

Mediterranean Pasta Salad

Makes 6 to 8 servings

½ box multigrain or whole wheat rigatoni or penne (about 7 ounces)

1 can (14 ounces) artichoke hearts in water, drained and cut into quarters

½ cup oil-packed sun-dried tomatoes, drained and chopped

¼ cup chopped fresh basil

½ cup sliced black olives

4 ounces feta cheese with sun-dried tomatoes and basil

½ cup balsamic, white balsamic or red wine vinegar

3 tablespoons olive oil

2 cloves garlic, minced

½ teaspoon salt

½ teaspoon dried oregano

¼ teaspoon black pepper

3 cups fresh baby spinach, stemmed and torn

¼ cup toasted pine nuts

1. Cook pasta according to package directions. Rinse under cold water until cool; drain well. Place in large bowl. Add artichokes, tomatoes, basil, olives and feta.

2. Whisk vinegar, oil, garlic, salt, oregano and pepper in small bowl until well blended.

3. Add spinach, dressing and pine nuts to salad just before serving. Toss gently.

TIP: To toast pine nuts, heat small nonstick skillet over medium heat. Add pine nuts. Cook 2 to 3 minutes or until lightly browned, stirring constantly. Remove immediately to plate to cool.

Vegetable Pasta Salad

Makes 8 servings

8 ounces uncooked rotini

4 cups broccoli florets

2 cups carrot slices

1½ cups chopped tomatoes

½ cup chopped green onions

1 cup mayonnaise

2 tablespoons white wine vinegar

1 tablespoon extra virgin olive oil

1 tablespoon minced fresh basil *or* 1 teaspoon dried basil

2 teaspoons minced fresh oregano *or* ½ teaspoon dried oregano

1 clove garlic, minced

1 teaspoon sugar

1 teaspoon dry mustard

½ teaspoon salt

¼ teaspoon black pepper

¼ cup grated Romano cheese

1. Cook pasta according to package directions. Rinse under cold water until cool; drain well. Place in large bowl.

2. Place steamer basket in large saucepan. Add water to saucepan not touching steamer basket. Add broccoli; steam 3 minutes or until crisp-tender. Immediately drain and run under cold water. Steam carrots 4 minutes or until crisp-tender; immediately drain and run under cold water. Add broccoli, carrots, tomatoes and green onions to pasta.

3. Whisk mayonnaise, vinegar, oil, basil, oregano, garlic, sugar, mustard, salt and pepper in medium bowl. Stir into pasta mixture. Add cheese; toss well. Refrigerate 3 hours or overnight to allow flavors to blend.

NOODLE SOUPS

Spinach Noodle Bowl with Ginger

Makes 4 servings

6   cups (48 ounces) chicken broth

4   ounces uncooked vermicelli noodles, broken into thirds

1½ cups matchstick carrots

3   ounces snow peas, cut in half and stems removed

4   cups packed spinach leaves (4 ounces)

1½ cups cooked shrimp or chicken

½   cup finely chopped green onions

1   tablespoon grated fresh ginger

1   teaspoon soy sauce

⅛   to ¼ teaspoon red pepper flakes

1. Bring broth to a boil in Dutch oven over high heat. Add vermicelli; return to a boil. Cook until al dente, about 2 minutes less than package instructions. Add carrots and snow peas; cook 2 minutes or until pasta is tender.

2. Remove from heat; stir in spinach, shrimp, green onions, ginger, soy sauce and red pepper flakes. Let stand 2 minutes before serving.

Minestrone Soup

Makes 4 to 6 servings

1 tablespoon olive oil

½ cup chopped onion

1 stalk celery, diced

1 carrot, diced

2 cloves garlic, minced

2 cups vegetable broth

1½ cups water

1 bay leaf

¾ teaspoon salt

½ teaspoon dried basil

½ teaspoon dried oregano

¼ teaspoon dried thyme

¼ teaspoon sugar

Black pepper

1 can (15 ounces) red kidney beans, rinsed and drained

1 can (15 ounces) navy beans, rinsed and drained

1 can (about 14 ounces) diced tomatoes

1 cup diced zucchini

½ cup uncooked small shell pasta

½ cup frozen cut green beans

¼ cup dry red wine

1 cup packed chopped fresh spinach

Grated Parmesan cheese

1. Heat oil in large saucepan or Dutch oven over medium-high heat. Add onion, celery, carrot and garlic; cook and stir 5 to 7 minutes or until vegetables are tender. Add broth, water, bay leaf, salt, basil, oregano, thyme, sugar and pepper; bring to a boil.

2. Stir in kidney beans, navy beans, tomatoes, zucchini, pasta, green beans and wine; cook 10 minutes, stirring occasionally.

3. Add spinach; cook 2 minutes or until pasta and zucchini are tender. Ladle into bowls; garnish with cheese.

Five-Way Cincinnati Chili

Makes 6 servings

1   pound uncooked spaghetti, broken in half

1   pound ground beef chuck

2   cans (10 ounces each) diced tomatoes with green chiles

1   can (15 ounces) red kidney beans, drained

1   can (10½ ounces) condensed French onion soup, undiluted

1¼   cups water

1   tablespoon chili powder

1   teaspoon sugar

½   teaspoon salt

¼   teaspoon ground cinnamon

½   cup chopped onion

½   cup (2 ounces) shredded Cheddar cheese

1. Cook pasta according to package directions; drain.

2. Meanwhile, brown beef in large saucepan or Dutch oven over medium-high heat 6 to 8 minutes, stirring to separate meat; drain well.

3. Add tomatoes, beans, soup, water, chili powder, sugar, salt and cinnamon to saucepan; bring to a boil. Reduce heat to low. Simmer, uncovered, 10 minutes, stirring occasionally.

4. Serve chili over spaghetti; sprinkle with onion and cheese.

NOTE: The ways of Cincinnati chili are: two-way over spaghetti, three-way with cheese, four-way with cheese and chopped onion and five-way with beans added to the chili.

Spicy Lentil and Pasta Soup

Makes 4 to 6 servings

1 tablespoon olive oil

2 medium onions, thinly sliced

½ cup chopped carrot

½ cup chopped celery

½ cup chopped peeled turnip

1 jalapeño pepper, seeded and finely chopped

2 cups water

2 cans (about 14 ounces each) vegetable broth

1 can (about 14 ounces) stewed tomatoes

8 ounces dried lentils, rinsed, sorted and drained

2 teaspoons chili powder

½ teaspoon salt

½ teaspoon dried oregano

3 ounces uncooked whole wheat spaghetti, broken into pieces

¼ cup minced fresh cilantro

1. Heat oil in large saucepan over medium heat. Add onions, carrot, celery, turnip and jalapeño; cook and stir 10 minutes or until vegetables are crisp-tender.

2. Add water, broth, tomatoes, lentils, chili powder, salt and oregano; bring to a boil. Reduce heat; cover and simmer 20 to 30 minutes or until lentils are tender.

3. Add pasta; cook 10 minutes or until tender. Ladle soup into bowls; sprinkle with cilantro.

Chicken and Gnocchi Soup

Makes 6 to 8 servings

¼ cup (½ stick) butter

1 tablespoon extra virgin olive oil

1 cup finely diced onion

2 stalks celery, finely chopped

2 cloves garlic, minced

¼ cup all-purpose flour

4 cups half-and-half

1 can (about 14 ounces) chicken broth

1 teaspoon salt

½ teaspoon dried thyme

½ teaspoon dried parsley flakes

¼ teaspoon ground nutmeg

1 package (about 16 ounces) gnocchi

1 package (6 ounces) fully cooked chicken strips, chopped *or* 1 cup diced cooked chicken

1 cup shredded carrots

1 cup coarsely chopped fresh spinach

1. Melt butter in large saucepan or Dutch oven over medium heat; add oil. Add onion, celery and garlic; cook about 10 minutes or until vegetables are softened and onion is translucent, stirring occasionally.

2. Whisk in flour; cook and stir about 1 minute. Whisk in half-and-half; cook about 15 minutes or until thickened.

3. Whisk in broth, salt, thyme, parsley flakes and nutmeg; cook 10 minutes or until slightly thickened. Add gnocchi, chicken, carrots and spinach; cook about 5 minutes or until gnocchi is heated through.

Chicken Noodle Soup

Makes 8 servings

2 tablespoons butter

1 cup chopped onion

1 cup sliced carrots

½ cup diced celery

2 tablespoons vegetable oil

1 pound chicken breast
  tenderloins

1 pound chicken thigh fillets

4 cups chicken broth, divided

2 cups water

1 tablespoon minced fresh
  parsley, plus additional for
  garnish

1½ teaspoons salt

½ teaspoon black pepper

3 cups uncooked egg noodles

1. Melt butter in large saucepan or Dutch oven over medium-low heat. Add onion, carrots and celery; cook 15 minutes or until vegetables are soft, stirring occasionally.

2. Meanwhile, heat oil in large skillet over medium-high heat. Add chicken in single layer; cook about 12 minutes or until lightly browned and cooked through, turning once. Transfer chicken to cutting board. Add 1 cup broth to skillet; cook 1 minute, scraping up any browned bits from bottom of skillet. Add broth to vegetables. Stir in remaining 3 cups broth, water, 1 tablespoon parsley, salt and pepper.

3. Chop chicken into 1-inch pieces when cool enough to handle. Add to soup; bring to a boil over medium-high heat. Reduce heat to medium-low; cook 15 minutes. Add noodles; cook 15 minutes or until noodles are tender. Ladle into bowls; garnish with additional parsley.

Vietnamese Beef and Noodle Soup

Makes 2 servings

4 cups water

2 ounces whole wheat angel hair pasta, broken in half

2¼ cups beef stock

1 shallot, sliced

1 whole star anise

½ teaspoon minced fresh ginger

1 teaspoon fish sauce or soy sauce

1 teaspoon soy sauce

½ teaspoon hot pepper sauce

6 ounces boneless beef sirloin, sliced ⅛ inch thick

½ teaspoon salt

⅛ teaspoon black pepper

1 cup bean sprouts

2 green onions, thinly sliced

1 small fresh red chile pepper, thinly sliced

2 tablespoons minced fresh cilantro

2 lime wedges

1. Bring water to a boil in small saucepan. Add pasta; cook 3 to 4 minutes or until tender. Drain; set aside.

2. Bring stock, shallot, star anise and ginger to a boil in medium saucepan. Reduce heat; simmer 10 minutes. Strain liquid into large saucepan; stir in fish sauce, soy sauce and hot pepper sauce.

3. Season beef with salt and black pepper. Add beef and bean sprouts to stock mixture; cook 1 to 2 minutes or until beef is no longer pink. Stir in cooked pasta and green onions.

4. Ladle soup into 2 bowls; top with chile slices and cilantro. Squeeze lime wedge over each serving.

Pasta Fagioli

Makes 8 servings

2 tablespoons olive oil, divided

1 pound ground beef

1 cup chopped onion

1 cup diced carrots (about 2 medium)

1 cup diced celery (about 2 stalks)

3 cloves garlic, minced

4 cups beef broth

1 can (28 ounces) diced tomatoes

1 can (15 ounces) tomato sauce

1 tablespoon cider vinegar

2 teaspoons sugar

1½ teaspoons dried basil

1¼ teaspoons salt

1 teaspoon dried oregano

¾ teaspoon dried thyme

2 cups uncooked ditalini pasta

1 can (15 ounces) red kidney beans, rinsed and drained

1 can (15 ounces) cannellini beans, rinsed and drained

Grated Romano cheese

1. Heat 1 tablespoon oil in large saucepan or Dutch oven over medium-high heat. Add beef; cook 5 minutes or until browned, stirring to break up meat. Transfer to medium bowl; set aside. Drain fat from saucepan.

2. Heat remaining 1 tablespoon oil in same saucepan over medium-high heat. Add onion, carrots and celery; cook and stir 5 minutes or until vegetables are tender. Add garlic; cook and stir 1 minute. Add cooked beef, broth, tomatoes, tomato sauce, vinegar, sugar, basil, salt, oregano and thyme; bring to a boil. Reduce heat to medium-low; cover and simmer 30 minutes.

3. Add pasta, kidney beans and cannellini beans; cook over medium heat 10 minutes or until pasta is tender, stirring frequently. Ladle into bowls; garnish with cheese.

Pasta and Bean Soup

Makes 6 servings

1¼ cups dried navy beans

6 cups cold water

3 slices bacon, finely chopped

1 onion, chopped

1 stalk celery, chopped

12 ounces smoked pork rib or neck bones

2 cloves garlic, minced

1 teaspoon salt

½ teaspoon dried thyme

½ teaspoon dried marjoram leaves, crushed

¼ teaspoon black pepper

¾ cup uncooked small pasta shells

2 tablespoons chopped fresh parsley

1 cup beef broth (optional)

Grated Parmesan cheese

1. Rinse beans in colander under cold water, picking out any debris or blemished beans. Combine beans and water in large saucepan. Cover and bring to a boil over high heat. Remove cover and boil 2 minutes. Remove from heat; cover and let stand 1 hour. Do not drain.

2. Cook bacon in medium skillet over medium-high heat 2 minutes. Add onion and celery; cook and stir 6 minutes or until golden brown. Add bacon and vegetables to beans. Add pork bones, garlic, salt, thyme, marjoram and pepper. Bring to a boil over high heat; reduce heat to medium-low. Simmer 1 hour or until beans are tender, stirring occasionally. Remove from heat.

3. Remove bones to plate; set aside.

4. Transfer half of bean mixture to food processor or blender. with slotted spoon. Add 2 tablespoons cooking liquid; process until smooth. Stir back into soup.

5. Bring to a boil over high heat. Stir in pasta. Reduce heat to medium-low; simmer, uncovered, 10 minutes or until pasta is tender, stirring occasionally.

6. Meanwhile, remove meat from bones; discard bones. Chop meat. Stir meat and parsley into soup. If soup is too thick, stir in beef broth until desired consistency. Serve with cheese.

Asian Pork and Noodle Soup

Makes 6 servings

2   cans (about 14 ounces each) chicken broth

¼   cup hoisin sauce

2   tablespoons chopped fresh ginger

2   tablespoons soy sauce

2   tablespoons unseasoned rice vinegar

2   tablespoons honey

2   cloves garlic, minced

1   pound pork tenderloin

1   pound baby bok choy, sliced

1   cup sliced shiitake mushrooms

8   ounces uncooked rice noodles

¼   cup chopped peanuts

SLOW COOKER DIRECTIONS

1. Whisk broth, hoisin sauce, ginger, soy sauce, vinegar, honey and garlic in slow cooker until smooth and well blended. Place pork in slow cooker. Cover; cook on LOW 6 hours.

2. Remove pork from slow cooker; set aside. Add bok choy, mushrooms and noodles to slow cooker, making sure noodles are submerged in liquid. Cover; cook 20 to 30 minutes.

3. When pork is cool enough to handle, shred with 2 forks. Stir into slow cooker; cook until heated through.

4. Ladle soup into bowls; top with peanuts.

EASY NOODLE DINNERS

Hearty Noodle Casserole

Makes 4 to 6 servings

1 pound Italian sausage, casings removed

1 jar (26 ounces) pasta sauce

2 cups (16 ounces) ricotta cheese

1 package (12 ounces) extra wide egg noodles, cooked and drained

2 cups (8 ounces) shredded mozzarella cheese, divided

1 can (4 ounces) sliced mushrooms, drained

½ cup chopped green bell pepper

1. Preheat oven to 350°F. Brown sausage in large skillet over medium-high heat 6 to 8 minutes, stirring to break up meat. Drain fat.

2. Combine sausage, pasta sauce, ricotta cheese, noodles, half of mozzarella cheese, mushrooms and bell pepper in large bowl. Spoon into 13×9-inch or 3-quart baking dish. Top with remaining mozzarella cheese.

3. Bake 25 minutes or until heated through.

Chicken Marsala with Fettuccine

Makes 6 servings

4 boneless skinless chicken breasts

Salt and black pepper

1 tablespoon vegetable oil

1 onion, chopped

½ cup marsala wine

2 packages (8 ounces each) sliced cremini mushrooms

½ cup chicken broth

2 teaspoons Worcestershire sauce

½ cup whipping cream

2 tablespoons cornstarch

8 ounces uncooked fettuccine

2 tablespoons chopped fresh Italian parsley

SLOW COOKER DIRECTIONS

1. Coat slow cooker with nonstick cooking spray. Place chicken in slow cooker; season with salt and pepper.

2. Heat oil in large skillet over medium heat. Add onion; cook and stir 2 minutes or until translucent. Add marsala; cook 2 to 3 minutes or until slightly thickened. Stir in mushrooms, broth and Worcestershire sauce. Pour mixture over chicken. Cover; cook on HIGH 1½ to 1¾ hours or until chicken is no longer pink in center.

3. Transfer chicken to cutting board; cover and keep warm. Stir cream into cornstarch in small bowl until smooth; stir into cooking liquid. Cover; cook 15 minutes or until thickened. Season with salt and pepper.

4. Meanwhile, cook pasta according to package directions. Drain well; transfer to large serving bowl. Slice chicken and place on pasta. Top with sauce; sprinkle with parsley.

Cheddar Tuna Noodles

Makes 4 to 6 servings

2 tablespoons butter

½ cup chopped onion

½ cup chopped celery

2 tablespoons all-purpose flour

½ teaspoon salt

¼ teaspoon red pepper flakes

2 cups milk

8 ounces egg noodles, cooked and drained

2 cans (6 ounces each) white tuna packed in water, drained and flaked

1 cup frozen peas

½ cup (2 ounces) shredded Cheddar cheese

1. Preheat oven to 375°F. Spray 9-inch square baking dish with nonstick cooking spray.

2. Melt butter in large skillet over medium heat. Add onion; cook and stir 3 minutes. Add celery; cook and stir 3 minutes.

3. Sprinkle flour, salt and red pepper flakes over onion mixture; cook and stir 2 minutes. Gradually whisk in milk; bring to a boil. Cook and stir 2 minutes or until thickened. Remove from heat.

4. Combine noodles, white sauce, tuna and peas in prepared baking dish; Stir to coat. Sprinkle with cheese. Bake 20 to 25 minutes or until bubbly.

Reuben Noodle Bake

Makes 6 servings

8 ounces uncooked egg noodles

5 ounces thinly sliced deli-style corned beef

2 cups (8 ounces) shredded Swiss cheese

1 can (about 14 ounces) sauerkraut with caraway seeds, drained

½ cup Thousand Island dressing

½ cup milk

1 tablespoon prepared mustard

2 slices pumpernickel bread

1 tablespoon butter, melted

1. Preheat oven to 350°F. Spray 13×9-inch baking dish with nonstick cooking spray. Cook noodles according to package directions; drain.

2. Meanwhile, cut corned beef into bite-size pieces. Combine noodles, corned beef, cheese and sauerkraut in large bowl. Transfer to prepared baking dish.

3. Combine dressing, milk and mustard in small bowl. Spoon evenly over noodle mixture.

4. Tear bread into large pieces; process in food processor or blender until crumbs form. Add butter; pulse to combine. Sprinkle over casserole.

5. Bake 25 to 30 minutes or until heated through.

Summer Spaghetti

Makes 4 to 6 servings

1 pound plum tomatoes, seeded and coarsely chopped

1 medium onion, chopped

⅓ cup chopped fresh parsley

6 pitted green olives, chopped

2 cloves garlic, minced

2 tablespoons finely shredded fresh basil

2 teaspoons drained capers

½ teaspoon salt

½ teaspoon paprika

¼ teaspoon dried oregano

1 tablespoon red wine vinegar

½ cup olive oil

1 pound uncooked spaghetti

Salt and black pepper

1. Combine tomatoes, onion, parsley, olives, garlic, basil, capers, ½ teaspoon salt, paprika and oregano in medium bowl; mix well. Drizzle with vinegar. Add oil; stir until well blended. Cover and let stand at room temperature 2 to 6 hours.

2. Cook pasta according to package directions; drain. Toss hot pasta with tomato mixture. Season with additional salt and pepper. Serve immediately.

Bow Tie Pasta with Chicken and Roasted Garlic

Makes 6 servings

1 head garlic

3 tablespoons plus 1 teaspoon olive oil, divided

Salt and black pepper

1 pound uncooked bowtie pasta

1½ pounds assorted mushrooms (such as shiitake, portobello or cremini), sliced

1 can (about 14 ounces) diced tomatoes, undrained

¾ cup chopped green onions

1½ cups chicken broth

1½ pounds cooked boneless skinless chicken breasts, diced

¼ cup chopped fresh cilantro

2 teaspoons salt

1 teaspoon black pepper

1. Preheat oven to 325°F. Cut off ¼ inch of garlic top. Place garlic on sheet of foil; drizzle with 1 teaspoon oil and season with salt and pepper. Bake 45 minutes or until garlic is soft. Unwrap and let stand until cool enough to handle. Squeeze garlic pulp into small bowl, set aside.

2. Cook pasta according to package directions; drain and place in large bowl.

3. Heat remaining 3 tablespoons oil in large skillet over medium-high heat. Add mushrooms; cook and stir 3 minutes. Add tomatoes and green onions; cook and stir 2 minutes. Add broth; simmer 5 minutes or until broth reduces to 1 cup. Add garlic, chicken, cilantro, 2 teaspoons salt and 1 teaspoon pepper; cook 2 minutes.

4. Add sauce to pasta; stir gently.

Kale, Gorgonzola and Noodle Casserole

Makes 6 servings

1 large bunch kale, stems removed, coarsely chopped (about 8 cups)

6 ounces uncooked egg noodles or fettuccine

2 tablespoons butter

1 clove garlic, crushed

¼ cup chopped green onions

2 tablespoons all-purpose flour

2¼ cups half-and-half

4 ounces gorgonzola cheese, crumbled

4 ounces fontina cheese, cut into small chunks

½ teaspoon salt

¼ teaspoon black pepper

¼ teaspoon ground nutmeg

¼ cup coarse dry bread crumbs

1. Preheat oven to 350°F. Spray 9-inch square baking dish with nonstick cooking spray.

2. Place kale in large saucepan with 1 inch of water. Cover; bring to a simmer. Steam kale 15 minutes or until tender. Drain well, pressing out excess liquid. Set aside.

3. Meanwhile, cook pasta according to package directions; drain.

4. Melt butter in large saucepan or deep skillet over medium-low heat. Add garlic and green onions; cook and stir over low heat 5 minutes. Discard garlic. Whisk in flour until paste forms. Gradually whisk in half-and-half. Cook until mixture thickens, stirring frequently. Gradually add cheeses until melted. Stir in salt, pepper and nutmeg. Stir in noodles and kale; mix well.

5. Spoon into prepared baking dish. Sprinkle with bread crumbs. Bake 30 minutes or until bubbly.

Classic Beef and Noodles

Makes 8 servings

1 tablespoon vegetable oil

2 pounds beef for stew, cut into 1-inch pieces

½ cup chopped onion

2 cloves garlic, minced

1 teaspoon salt

1 teaspoon dried oregano

½ teaspoon black pepper

¼ teaspoon dried marjoram

8 ounces mushrooms, halved

1½ cups beef broth

⅓ cup dry sherry

1 bay leaf

1 cup (8 ounces) sour cream

½ cup all-purpose flour

¼ cup water

4 cups hot cooked egg noodles

Chopped fresh parsley

SLOW COOKER DIRECTIONS

1. Heat oil in large skillet. Brown beef on all sides, working in batches, if necessary. Drain fat.

2. Transfer beef to slow cooker. Add onion to skillet; cook and stir 5 minutes or until softened. Add garlic, salt, oregano, pepper and marjoram; cook and stir 1 minute. Transfer mixture to slow cooker. Add mushrooms, broth, sherry and bay leaf.

3. Cover; cook on LOW 8 to 10 hours or on HIGH 4 to 5 hours. Remove and discard bay leaf.

4. Combine sour cream, flour and water in small bowl. Stir about 1 cup liquid from slow cooker into sour cream mixture. Add mixture to slow cooker. Cook, uncovered, on HIGH 30 minutes or until thickened and bubbly. Serve over noodles. Garnish with parsley.

Penne Chicken Casserole

Makes 6 servings

1½ pounds boneless skinless chicken breasts

3 cups water

2 beef or chicken bouillon cubes

4 cups cooked penne pasta

1 can (10¾ ounces) condensed cream of chicken soup, undiluted

1 cup sour cream

½ cup grated Asiago cheese

½ cup mayonnaise

⅓ cup dry sherry

½ cup Italian-seasoned dry bread crumbs

¼ cup grated Parmesan cheese

¼ cup (½ stick) butter, melted

1. Preheat oven to 350°F. Spray 2-quart baking dish with nonstick cooking spray.

2. Place chicken, water and bouillon cubes in large saucepan over medium heat. Cook 20 minutes or until chicken is no longer pink in center. Drain liquid and discard; cut chicken into cubes. Combine pasta and chicken in prepared baking dish.

3. Combine soup, sour cream, Asiago cheese, mayonnaise and sherry in medium bowl; mix well. Spoon evenly over pasta and chicken.

4. Toss bread crumbs, Parmesan cheese and butter in small bowl. Sprinkle over casserole. Bake 30 to 45 minutes or until top is golden brown.

Ravioli-Style Casserole

Makes 8 to 10 servings

1 pound ground beef

2 tablespoons dried onion flakes

2 teaspoons soy sauce

1 clove garlic, minced

2 packages (10 ounces each) frozen chopped spinach, thawed and drained

1 jar (26 ounces) marinara sauce

1 can (8 ounces) tomato sauce

1 can (6 ounces) tomato paste

1 tablespoon barbecue sauce

½ teaspoon dried oregano

¼ teaspoon black pepper

8 ounces uncooked elbow macaroni, cooked and drained

2 cups (8 ounces) shredded sharp Cheddar cheese

½ cup plain dry bread crumbs

2 eggs, beaten

Grated Parmesan cheese

1. Preheat oven to 350°F. Spray 13×9-inch baking dish with nonstick cooking spray.

2. Cook ground beef, onion, soy sauce and garlic in large skillet over medium heat 5 minutes or until no longer pink. Stir in spinach, marinara sauce, tomato sauce, tomato paste, barbecue sauce, oregano and pepper. Reduce heat to low; simmer 10 minutes.

3. Combine macaroni, Cheddar cheese, bread crumbs and eggs in large bowl; mix well. Spread evenly into bottom of prepared casserole; top with beef mixture. Cover loosely with foil.

4. Bake 30 minutes or until hot and bubbly, removing foil during the last 10 minutes of baking. Sprinkle with Parmesan cheese.

Tuna Noodle Bake

Makes 6 to 8 servings

4 tablespoons butter, divided

1 small onion, finely chopped

2 cloves garlic, minced

2 tablespoons all-purpose flour

1½ cups milk

1 teaspoon Italian seasoning

½ teaspoon salt

½ teaspoon black pepper

½ teaspoon dry mustard

½ teaspoon dried thyme

4 cups cooked elbow macaroni, rotini or other small pasta shape

2 cans (6 ounces each) tuna, drained and flaked

2 cups peas

½ cup crushed potato chips

1. Preheat oven to 350°F. Melt 2 tablespoons butter in small skillet. Add onion and garlic; cook and stir 2 minutes or until softened.

2. Melt remaining 2 tablespoons butter in medium saucepan over low heat. Whisk in flour; cook and stir 2 minutes without browning. Gradually whisk in milk; bring to a boil. Reduce heat; simmer 2 to 3 minutes or until thickened. Stir in Italian seasoning, salt, pepper, mustard and thyme.

3. Combine pasta, onion mixture, tuna and peas in large bowl. Add sauce; mix well. Transfer to 2-quart or 13×9-inch baking dish. Sprinkle with potato chips.

4. Cover; bake 15 minutes. Uncover; bake 10 minutes or until hot and bubbly.

Skillet Vegetable Lasagna

Makes 6 servings

8 ounces hot Italian turkey sausage, casings removed

8 ounces ground turkey

2 stalks celery, sliced

⅓ cup chopped onion

2 cups marinara sauce

1⅓ cups water

4 ounces uncooked bowtie (farfalle) pasta

1 medium zucchini, halved lengthwise and cut into ½-inch-thick slices (2 cups)

¾ cup chopped green or yellow bell pepper

½ cup (2 ounces) shredded mozzarella cheese

½ cup ricotta cheese

2 tablespoons finely grated Parmesan cheese

1. Heat large skillet over medium-high heat. Add sausage, ground turkey, celery and onion; cook and stir 6 to 8 minutes or until turkey is no longer pink. Stir in marinara sauce and water; bring to a boil. Stir in pasta. Reduce heat to medium-low; cover and simmer 12 minutes.

2. Stir in zucchini and bell pepper; cover and simmer 2 minutes. Uncover and simmer 4 to 6 minutes or until vegetables are crisp-tender.

3. Sprinkle with mozzarella cheese. Combine ricotta and Parmesan cheeses in small bowl; stir to blend. Drop by rounded teaspoonfuls on top of mixture in skillet. Remove from heat; cover and let stand 10 minutes.

Fusilli Pizzaiolo

Makes 6 to 8 servings

1 package (16 ounces) uncooked fusilli or rotini pasta

¼ cup olive oil

8 ounces mushrooms, sliced

1 red bell pepper, chopped

1 green bell pepper, chopped

1 yellow bell pepper, chopped

3 large shallots, chopped

10 green onions, chopped

1 large onion, chopped

8 cloves garlic, minced

½ cup chopped fresh basil *or* 2 teaspoons dried basil

2 tablespoons chopped fresh oregano *or* 1 teaspoon dried oregano, crushed

Dash red pepper flakes

4 cups canned or fresh tomatoes, undrained and chopped

Salt and black pepper

1. Cook pasta according to package directions. Drain and keep warm.

2. Heat oil in large skillet over medium-high heat. Add mushrooms, bell peppers, shallots, green onions and garlic; cook and stir 5 minutes or until vegetables are lightly browned. Stir in basil, oregano and red pepper flakes.

3. Add tomatoes with juice; bring to a boil. Reduce heat to low; simmer, uncovered, 20 minutes. Season to taste with salt and black pepper.

4. Add pasta to sauce; toss to coat.

Cheesy Spinach Bake

Makes 4 servings

8 ounces uncooked spinach fettuccine

1 tablespoon vegetable oil

1½ cups sliced mushrooms

2 green onions, finely chopped

1 teaspoon garlic, minced

1 package (10 ounces) frozen spinach, thawed and drained*

2 tablespoons water

1 container (15 ounces) ricotta cheese

¾ cup whipping cream

1 egg

½ teaspoon salt

½ teaspoon ground nutmeg

½ teaspoon black pepper

½ cup (2 ounces) shredded Swiss cheese

Or substitute 10 ounces coarsely chopped fresh baby spinach.

1. Preheat oven to 350°F. Spray 1½-quart baking dish with nonstick cooking spray. Cook pasta according to package directions; drain.

2. Heat oil in medium skillet over medium heat. Add mushrooms, green onions and garlic; cook and stir until mushrooms are softened. Add spinach and water. Cover and cook about 3 minutes or until spinach is wilted.

3. Combine ricotta cheese, cream, egg, salt, nutmeg and black pepper in large bowl. Gently stir in noodles and vegetables until blended. Spread noodle mixture in prepared baking dish. Sprinkle with Swiss cheese.

4. Bake 25 to 30 minutes or until knife inserted halfway into center comes out clean.

Baked Mostaccioli

Makes 8 servings

1 container (15 ounces) ricotta cheese

2 eggs, beaten

¼ cup grated Parmesan cheese

1 teaspoon garlic powder

½ teaspoon salt

½ teaspoon black pepper

½ teaspoon Italian seasoning

1 package (16 ounces) mostaccioli, cooked and drained

1 jar (26 ounces) prepared pasta sauce

1½ cups (6 ounces) shredded mozzarella cheese

1. Preheat oven to 350°F. Spray 13×9-inch baking dish with nonstick cooking spray.

2. Combine ricotta cheese, eggs and Parmesan cheese in medium bowl. Season with garlic powder, salt, pepper and Italian seasoning; mix well.

3. Place half of pasta and half of sauce in prepared casserole. Spread ricotta mixture evenly over pasta. Spoon remaining pasta and sauce over ricotta mixture. Top with mozzarella cheese.

4. Bake 30 minutes or until hot and bubbly.

Mushroom Spaghetti

Makes 2 to 4 servings

2 cups boiling water

1 package (1 ounce) dried porcini mushrooms

8 ounces whole wheat spaghetti

2 tablespoons butter

2 tablespoons olive oil

4 cloves garlic, minced

½ teaspoon salt

½ cup shredded Parmesan cheese

Chopped fresh parsley

1. Pour boiling water over mushrooms in medium bowl. Let stand 20 minute to soften. Remove mushrooms with slotted spoon; squeeze dry and coarsely chop. Strain soaking liquid through fine mesh sieve.

2. Meanwhile, cook pasta according to package directions. Drain and return to saucepan; keep warm.

3. Heat butter and oil in large skillet over medium-low heat until butter is melted. Add garlic; cook and stir 1 minute or until fragrant. Add mushrooms and salt; cook and stir 1 minute. Add pasta and about ¼ cup mushroom water; cook and stir until absorbed. Add additional water, if needed, until desired consistency is reached.

4. Transfer pasta to serving plates; top with cheese and parsley.

NOTE: If dried mushrooms are not available, substitute 8 ounces of sliced fresh mushrooms instead. In step 3, cook mushrooms in butter and oil for about 5 minutes or until tender and browned, stirring occasionally. Add garlic; cook and stir 1 minute. Reserve some of pasta cooking water and add to skillet with pasta instead of mushroom liquid.

MACARONI & CHEESE

Hearty Vegetarian Mac and Cheese

Makes 6 servings

1   can (about 14 ounces)
     stewed tomatoes,
     undrained

1½   cups prepared Alfredo sauce

1½   cups (6 ounces) shredded
     mozzarella cheese, divided

8   ounces whole grain shell
     pasta or penne, cooked and
     drained

7   ounces Italian-flavored
     vegetarian sausage links,
     cut into ¼-inch slices

¾   cup fresh basil leaves, thinly
     sliced, divided

½   cup vegetable broth

½   teaspoon salt

2   tablespoons grated
     Parmesan cheese

SLOW COOKER DIRECTIONS

1. Coat inside of slow cooker with nonstick cooking spray. Add tomatoes, Alfredo sauce, 1 cup mozzarella cheese, pasta, sausage, ½ cup basil, broth and salt to slow cooker; stir to blend. Top with remaining ½ cup mozzarella cheese and Parmesan cheese.

2. Cover; cook on LOW 3½ hours or on HIGH 2 hours. Top with remaining ¼ cup basil.

Southern Macaroni and Cheese

Makes 4 servings

2 tablespoons all-purpose flour

1½ tablespoons dry mustard

1 teaspoon salt

½ teaspoon black pepper

3 cups milk

2 cups (8 ounces) shredded sharp Cheddar cheese, divided

2 egg whites

4 cups cooked whole wheat or regular elbow macaroni

¼ cup panko or plain dry bread crumbs

½ teaspoon paprika

1. Preheat oven to 325°F. Spray 2-quart baking dish with nonstick cooking spray.

2. Combine flour, mustard, salt and pepper in medium saucepan; whisk in milk. Cook and stir over medium heat until mixture is bubbly and thickened. Remove from heat; let stand 2 to 3 minutes. Stir in 1½ cups cheese until melted.

3. Stir egg whites into macaroni in large bowl. Stir in cheese sauce. Spoon into prepared dish. Combine remaining ½ cup cheese, panko and paprika in small bowl; mix well. Sprinkle over macaroni.

4. Bake 15 to 20 minutes or until bubbly and lightly browned. Let stand 5 minutes before serving.

Cauliflower Mac and Gouda

Makes 8 to 10 servings

1 package (about 16 ounces) bowtie pasta

4 cups milk

2 cloves garlic, crushed

¼ cup (½ stick) plus 3 tablespoons butter, divided

5 tablespoons all-purpose flour

1 pound Gouda cheese, shredded

1 teaspoon dry mustard

⅛ teaspoon smoked paprika or paprika

Salt and black pepper

1 head cauliflower, cored and cut into florets

1 cup panko bread crumbs

1. Cook pasta according to package directions in large saucepan of boiling salted water until al dente. Drain pasta, reserving pasta water; keep warm. Return water to a boil.

2. Bring milk and garlic to a boil in small saucepan. Reduce heat; keep warm. Discard garlic.

3. Melt ¼ cup butter in large saucepan over medium heat; whisk in flour. Cook 1 minute, whisking constantly. Gradually whisk in milk in thin steady stream. Bring to a boil, whisking frequently. Reduce heat; cook and stir 10 minutes or until thickened. Remove from heat.

4. Add cheese, mustard and paprika to sauce mixture; whisk until melted. Season with salt and pepper. Keep warm.

5. Preheat broiler. Add cauliflower to boiling pasta water. Cook 3 to 5 minutes or just until tender; drain. Toss pasta and cauliflower with sauce mixture. Spoon pasta mixture into individual baking dishes or 13×9-inch baking dish.

6. Melt remaining 3 tablespoons butter in medium skillet. Add panko; cook and stir until golden brown. Sprinkle on individual servings.

Classic Macaroni and Cheese

Makes 6 servings

2 cups uncooked elbow macaroni

¼ cup (½ stick) butter

¼ cup all-purpose flour

2½ cups whole milk

1 teaspoon salt

⅛ teaspoon black pepper

4 cups (16 ounces) shredded Colby Jack cheese

1. Cook pasta according to package directions; drain.

2. Melt butter in large saucepan over medium heat. Add flour; whisk until well blended and bubbly. Gradually add milk, salt and pepper, whisking until blended. Cook and stir until milk begins to bubble. Add cheese, 1 cup at a time; cook and stir until cheese is melted and sauce is smooth.

3. Add cooked pasta; stir gently until blended. Cook until heated through.

Pesto Chicken Mac and Cheese

Makes 6 to 8 servings

- 4 cups milk
- 1 clove garlic, crushed
- ¼ cup (½ stick) butter
- 5 tablespoons all-purpose flour
- 8 ounces fontina cheese, shredded
- 2 cups (8 ounces) shredded mozzarella cheese
- ½ cup grated Parmesan cheese
- ½ cup pesto
  Salt and black pepper
- 1 package (16 ounces) radiatore or penne pasta, cooked and drained
- 1 pound chopped cooked chicken
- 1 package (about 5 ounces) baby spinach

1. Bring milk and garlic to a boil in small saucepan. Remove from heat; discard garlic.

2. Melt butter in large saucepan over medium heat; whisk in flour. Cook and stir 2 minutes. Gradually whisk in milk in thin steady stream. Bring to a boil. Reduce heat; cook and stir 10 minutes or until thickened. Remove from heat.

3. Add cheeses to sauce, whisking until smooth. Stir in pesto; season with salt and pepper. Toss pasta, chicken and spinach with pesto mixture until spinach wilts. Serve immediately.

Mediterranean Mac and Cheese

Makes 4 to 6 servings

8 ounces uncooked elbow macaroni or other small pasta shape

1 tablespoon olive oil

1 red bell pepper, cut into slivers

1 bunch (about ¾ pound) asparagus, cut into bite-size pieces

4 tablespoons butter, divided

¼ cup all-purpose flour

1¾ cups milk, heated

1 teaspoon minced fresh thyme

   Salt and black pepper

1 cup (4 ounces) shredded mozzarella cheese

1 cup chopped cooked chicken

4 ounces garlic and herb flavored goat cheese

¼ cup dry bread crumbs

1. Preheat oven to 350°F. Cook pasta according to package directions until almost al dente. Rinse under cold water until cool; drain well.

2. Meanwhile, heat oil in medium skillet over medium-high heat. Add bell pepper; cook and stir 3 minutes. Add asparagus; cook and stir 3 minutes or until crisp-tender. Remove from skillet.

3. Melt 3 tablespoons butter in large saucepan or deep skillet over medium heat. Whisk in flour until smooth paste forms; cook and stir 2 minutes without browning. Gradually whisk in milk in thin steady stream. Cook 6 to 8 minutes, whisking constantly until mixture begins to bubble and thickens slightly. Add thyme and season with salt and black pepper. Remove from heat.

4. Stir in mozzarella cheese until melted. Stir in pasta, vegetables and chicken. Crumble goat cheese into mixture; transfer to 2-quart baking dish. Top with bread crumbs and dot with remaining 1 tablespoon butter.

5. Bake 25 to 30 minutes or until lightly browned and bubbly.

Shells and Fontina

Makes 4 to 6 servings

8 ounces uncooked small shell pasta

1¾ cups milk

4 large fresh sage leaves

3 tablespoons butter

4 tablespoons all-purpose flour

½ cup tomato sauce

Salt and black pepper

¾ cup grated Parmesan cheese, divided

5½ ounces fontina cheese, shredded*

¼ cup plain dry bread crumbs

It is easier to shred fontina cheese if it is very cold. Keep it in the refrigerator or place it in the freezer for 10 minutes before shredding.

1. Preheat oven to 350°F. Cook pasta according to package directions until barely al dente. Rinse under cold water until cool; drain well.

2. Meanwhile, heat milk with sage leaves in small saucepan over medium heat (do not boil). Melt butter in large saucepan over medium heat until bubbly. Whisk in flour until smooth; cook and stir 2 minutes without browning. Remove sage and gradually whisk in milk in thin steady stream. Cook 4 to 5 minutes, whisking constantly until mixture begins to bubble and thickens slightly. Stir in tomato sauce; season with salt and pepper. Remove from heat; stir in ½ cup Parmesan cheese until smooth.

3. Add pasta to sauce; stir to coat. Spoon one third of pasta mixture into 2-quart casserole. Top with one third of shredded fontina cheese. Repeat layers twice. Sprinkle with bread crumbs and remaining ¼ cup Parmesan cheese.

4. Bake 20 to 25 minutes or until hot and bubbly.

Three-Cheese Macaroni and Quinoa

Makes 4 servings

4 tablespoons butter, divided

½ cup panko bread crumbs

2 quarts water

1 teaspoon salt, divided

6 ounces uncooked whole grain elbow macaroni (1½ cups)

½ cup uncooked quinoa

2 tablespoons all-purpose flour

1 cup milk

1 cup (4 ounces) shredded sharp Cheddar cheese

1 cup (4 ounces) shredded Monterey Jack cheese

¼ cup grated Parmesan cheese

1. Melt 2 tablespoons butter in medium saucepan over medium heat. Add panko; cook and stir 3 minutes or until golden. Transfer to small bowl; wipe out saucepan.

2. Combine water and ½ teaspoon salt in large saucepan; bring to a boil over high heat. Stir in macaroni and quinoa; cook 10 minutes. Drain in fine-mesh strainer. Place in large bowl.

3. Melt remaining 2 tablespoons butter in medium saucepan over medium heat. Whisk in flour; cook 1 minute without browning. Gradually whisk in milk in thin steady stream. Cook about 5 minutes or until very thick, stirring constantly. Stir in Cheddar and Monterey Jack cheeses and remaining ½ teaspoon salt until melted. Stir into macaroni mixture.

4. Top with Parmesan cheese and panko. Garnish as desired.

TIP: For a spicy flavor, try Pepper Jack cheese in place of the Monterey Jack.

Pumpkin Mac and Cheese

Makes 6 to 8 servings

1 package (16 ounces) uncooked large elbow macaroni

½ cup (1 stick) butter, divided

¼ cup all-purpose flour

1½ cups milk

1 teaspoon salt, divided

¼ teaspoon ground nutmeg

⅛ teaspoon ground red pepper

2 cups (8 ounces) shredded Cheddar cheese

1 cup (4 ounces) shredded Monterey Jack cheese

1 cup canned pumpkin

1 cup panko bread crumbs

½ cup chopped hazelnuts or walnuts (optional)

⅛ teaspoon dried sage

1 cup (4 ounces) shredded Chihuahua cheese*

*If Chihuahua cheese is not available, substitute Monterey Jack cheese.

1. Preheat oven to 350°F. Spray 2-quart baking dish with nonstick cooking spray. Cook macaroni according to package directions until barley al dente. Drain and return to saucepan; keep warm.

2. Melt ¼ cup butter in medium saucepan over medium-high heat. Whisk in flour until smooth; cook 1 minute without browning, whisking constantly. Gradually whisk in milk in thin steady stream. Add ¾ teaspoon salt, nutmeg and red pepper; cook 2 to 3 minutes or until thickened, stirring frequently. Gradually add Cheddar and Monterey Jack cheeses, stirring after each addition until smooth. Add pumpkin; cook 1 minute or until heated through, stirring constantly. Pour sauce over pasta; stir to coat.

3. Melt remaining ¼ cup butter in small skillet over medium-low heat; cook until golden brown. Remove from heat; stir in panko, hazelnuts, if desired, sage and remaining ¼ teaspoon salt.

4. Spread half of pasta in prepared baking dish; sprinkle with ½ cup Chihuahua cheese. Top with remaining pasta; sprinkle with remaining Chihuahua cheese. Top with panko mixture.

5. Bake 25 to 30 minutes or until topping is golden brown and pasta is heated through.

Roasted Garlic and Stout Mac and Cheese

Makes 8 to 10 servings

1   head garlic

1   tablespoon olive oil

6   tablespoons (¾ stick) butter, divided

1   cup panko bread crumbs

1¼ teaspoons salt, divided

¼   cup all-purpose flour

½   teaspoon black pepper

2   cups whole milk

¾   cup Irish stout

2   cups (8 ounces) shredded sharp Cheddar cheese

2   cups (8 ounces) shredded Dubliner cheese

1   pound cellentani pasta,* cooked and drained

*Or substitute elbow macaroni, penne or other favorite pasta shape.

1. Preheat oven to 375°F. Spray 4-quart shallow baking dish with nonstick cooking spray.

2. Place garlic on 10-inch piece of foil; drizzle with oil and wrap loosely. Bake 30 minutes or until tender. Let stand until cool enough to handle. Squeeze cloves into small bowl; mash into smooth paste.

3. Melt 2 tablespoons butter in medium skillet over medium heat. Stir in panko and ¼ teaspoon salt. Set aside.

4. Melt remaining 4 tablespoons butter in large saucepan over medium heat. Add flour; cook and stir until lightly browned. Stir in roasted garlic paste, remaining 1 teaspoon salt and pepper. Slowly whisk in milk and stout in thin steady stream. Cook 3 to 5 minutes or until thickened, stirring frequently. Remove from heat; whisk in cheeses, ½ cup at a time, until melted. Combine cheese mixture and pasta in large bowl. Spoon into prepared baking dish; sprinkle with panko mixture.

5. Bake 40 minutes or until bubbly and topping is golden brown. Let stand 10 minutes before serving.

Mac and Cheese Pizza

Makes 4 to 6 servings

1½ tablespoons butter

1½ tablespoons all-purpose flour

1 cup half-and-half or milk

¼ teaspoon salt

¼ teaspoon black pepper

¼ teaspoon dried oregano

½ cup shredded fontina cheese

½ cup shredded Parmesan cheese

3 cups cooked* elbow macaroni (about 1½ cups uncooked)

1 tablespoon olive oil

1 cup sliced mushrooms

8 ounces sweet Italian sausage, casings removed

1 cup marinara sauce

1 cup (4 ounces) shredded mozzarella cheese

Cook macaroni until very tender, a bit longer than for al dente.

1. Preheat oven to 350°F. Spray 10-inch round deep-dish pizza pan, tart pan or baking dish with nonstick cooking spray.

2. Melt butter in large saucepan or deep skillet until bubbly over medium-low heat until bubbly. Whisk in flour until smooth paste forms. Gradually whisk in half-and-half in thin steady stream; cook until thickened, whisking frequently. Add salt, pepper and oregano. Gradually stir in fontina and Parmesan cheeses until melted. Stir in macaroni. Spoon into prepared pan. Press down firmly into even layer. Bake 15 minutes. Set aside.

3. Meanwhile, heat oil in large skillet over medium heat. Add mushrooms; cook 5 minutes, stirring occasionally. Add sausage; cook until browned, breaking into bite-size pieces with wooden spoon. Drain fat. Stir in marinara sauce; cook 1 minute or until heated through.

4. Spread sauce mixture evenly over macaroni layer. Sprinkle with mozzarella cheese. Bake 15 to 20 minutes or until sauce is bubbly and cheese is melted. Let stand 5 minutes before slicing.

Mac and Cheesiest

Makes about 6 servings

8 ounces uncooked elbow macaroni

¼ cup (½ stick) butter

5 tablespoons all-purpose flour

2¾ cups warm milk

1 teaspoon salt

¼ teaspoon ground nutmeg

¼ teaspoon black pepper

2 to 3 drops hot pepper sauce (optional)

8 ounces (about 2 cups) shredded Cheddar cheese, divided

2 ounces (about ½ cup) shredded Gruyère or Swiss cheese

2 ounces (about ½ cup) shredded American cheese

3 ounces (about ¾ cup) shredded aged Gouda cheese

1. Preheat oven to 350°F. Cook pasta according to package directions until barely al dente. Rinse under cold water until cool; drain well.

2. Melt butter in large saucepan or deep skillet over medium heat until bubbly. Whisk in flour until smooth; cook and stir 2 minutes without browning. Gradually whisk in milk in thin steady stream; cook 6 to 8 minutes, whisking constantly until mixture begins to bubble and thickens slightly. Add salt, nutmeg, black pepper and hot pepper sauce, if desired.

3. Remove from heat. Stir in 1½ cups Cheddar, Gruyère, American and Gouda cheeses until smooth. Stir pasta into cheese sauce. Transfer to 2-quart baking dish; sprinkle with remaining ½ cup Cheddar cheese.

4. Bake 20 to 30 minutes or until golden brown.

Cheddar and Cavatappi

Makes 4 to 6 servings

8 ounces uncooked whole wheat cavatappi pasta (about 3 cups)

6 tablespoons butter, divided

3 shallots, thinly sliced

5 tablespoons all-purpose flour

1 cup milk

1 cup whipping cream

½ teaspoon salt

½ teaspoon dry mustard

2 drops hot pepper sauce (optional)

3 cups (12 ounces) shredded Cheddar cheese

1 cup peas

¼ cup plain dry bread crumbs

1. Preheat oven to 350°F. Cook pasta according to package directions until barely al dente. Rinse under cold water until cool; drain well.

2. Meanwhile, melt 1 tablespoon butter in medium skillet over low heat. Add shallots; cook and stir 5 to 7 minutes or until well browned. Remove from heat.

3. Melt 4 tablespoons butter in large saucepan or deep skillet over medium heat until bubbly. Whisk in flour until smooth paste forms; cook and stir 2 minutes without browning. Gradually whisk in milk and cream in thin steady stream; cook 4 to 6 minutes, whisking frequently until mixture begins to bubble and thicken. Stir in salt, mustard and pepper sauce, if desired.

4. Turn heat to low; gradually stir in Cheddar cheese until melted. Remove from heat. Stir in pasta, shallots and peas.

5. Transfer to 1½-quart baking dish; sprinkle with bread crumbs. Bake 20 to 25 minutes or until hot and bubbly.

ASIAN NOODLES

Ginger Noodles with Sesame Egg Strips

Makes 4 servings

5 egg whites

6 teaspoons teriyaki sauce, divided

3 teaspoons sesame seeds, toasted,* divided

1 teaspoon dark sesame oil

½ cup vegetable broth

1 tablespoon minced fresh ginger

6 ounces Chinese rice noodles or vermicelli, cooked and well drained

⅓ cup sliced green onions

*To toast sesame seeds, spread seeds in small skillet. Shake skillet over medium heat 2 minutes or until seeds begin to pop and turn golden.

1. Beat egg whites, 2 teaspoons teriyaki sauce and 1 teaspoon sesame seeds in large bowl.

2. Heat oil in large nonstick skillet over medium heat. Pour egg mixture into skillet; cook 1½ to 2 minutes or until bottom is set. Turn over; cook 30 seconds to 1 minute or until cooked through. Gently slide onto plate; cut into ½-inch strips when cool enough to handle.

3. Add broth, ginger and remaining 4 teaspoons teriyaki sauce to skillet. Bring to a boil over high heat; reduce heat to medium. Add noodles; heat through. Add omelet strips and green onions; heat through. Sprinkle with remaining 2 teaspoons sesame seeds just before serving.

Cold Peanut Noodle and Edamame Salad

Makes 4 servings

½ (8-ounce) package brown rice pad thai noodles*

3 tablespoons soy sauce

2 tablespoons toasted sesame oil

2 tablespoons unseasoned rice vinegar

1 tablespoon sugar

1 tablespoon finely grated fresh ginger

1 tablespoon creamy peanut butter

1 tablespoon sriracha or hot chili sauce

2 teaspoons minced garlic

½ cup thawed frozen shelled edamame

¼ cup shredded carrots

¼ cup sliced green onions

Chopped peanuts (optional)

Brown rice pad thai noodles can be found in the Asian section of the supermarket. Four ounces whole wheat spaghetti may be substituted.

1. Cook noodles according to package directions. Rinse under cold water until cool; drain. Cut noodles into 3-inch lengths. Place in large bowl.

2. Whisk soy sauce, oil, vinegar, sugar, ginger, peanut butter, sriracha and garlic in small bowl until smooth and well blended.

3. Pour dressing over noodles; toss gently to coat. Stir in edamame and carrots. Cover and refrigerate at least 30 minutes before serving. Top with green onions and peanuts, if desired.

Asian Pesto Noodles

Makes 4 servings

3 cups fresh basil

3 cups fresh cilantro

3 cups fresh mint

¾ cup peanut oil

3 tablespoons sugar

2 to 3 tablespoons lime juice

5 cloves garlic, chopped

2 teaspoons fish sauce *or* 1 teaspoon salt

1 serrano pepper, finely chopped

1 pound large raw shrimp, peeled and deveined

12 ounces uncooked soba (buckwheat) noodles

1. Combine basil, cilantro, mint, oil, sugar, lime juice, garlic, fish sauce and pepper in food processor; process until well blended and finely chopped. Combine ¾ cup pesto and shrimp in medium bowl.

2. Cook soba noodles according to package directions; drain and set aside. Preheat broiler or grill.

3. Place marinated shrimp on metal skewers. (If using wooden skewers, soak in water for at least 30 minutes to prevent burning.) Place skewers under broiler or on grill; cook about 3 minutes per side or until shrimp are opaque.

4. To serve, toss soba noodles with remaining pesto. Serve with shrimp.

Soba Stir-Fry

Makes 4 servings

8 ounces uncooked soba (buckwheat) noodles

1 tablespoon olive oil

2 cups sliced shiitake mushrooms

1 medium red bell pepper, cut into thin strips

2 whole dried red chiles *or* ¼ teaspoon red pepper flakes

1 clove garlic, minced

2 cups shredded napa cabbage

½ cup vegetable broth

2 tablespoons tamari or soy sauce

1 tablespoon rice wine or dry sherry

2 teaspoons cornstarch

1 package (14 ounces) firm tofu, drained and cut into 1-inch cubes

Salt and black pepper

2 green onions, thinly sliced

1. Cook noodles according to package directions. Drain and set aside.

2. Heat oil in large nonstick skillet or wok over medium-high heat. Add mushrooms, bell pepper, dried chiles and garlic. Cook and stir 3 minutes or until mushrooms are tender. Add cabbage. Cover; cook 2 minutes or until cabbage is wilted.

3. Whisk broth, tamari and rice wine into cornstarch in small bowl until smooth. Stir sauce into vegetable mixture. Cook 2 minutes or until sauce is thickened.

4. Stir in tofu and noodles; toss gently until heated through. Season with salt and black pepper. Sprinkle with green onions. Serve immediately.

Rice Noodles with Broccoli and Tofu

Makes 4 to 6 servings

1 package (14 ounces) firm or extra firm tofu

1 package (8 to 10 ounces) wide rice noodles

2 tablespoons peanut oil

3 medium shallots, sliced

6 cloves garlic, minced

1 jalapeño pepper, minced

2 teaspoons minced fresh ginger

3 cups broccoli florets

3 tablespoons regular soy sauce

1 tablespoon sweet soy sauce (kecap manis)*

1 to 2 tablespoons fish sauce**

Fresh basil leaves (optional)

If sweet soy sauce is not available, substitute 1 tablespoon soy sauce plus 1 tablespoon packed brown sugar.

**To make this dish vegetarian, look for vegetarian fish sauce or substitute additional soy sauce or fresh lime juice.*

1. Cut tofu crosswise in half. Place tofu on cutting board between layers of paper towels; place weighted saucepan or baking dish on top of tofu. Let stand 30 minutes to drain. Place rice noodles in large bowl; cover with boiling water. Soak 30 minutes or until soft.

2. Cut tofu into bite-size squares and blot dry. Heat oil in large skillet or wok over medium-high heat. Add tofu to skillet; stir-fry about 5 minutes or until tofu is lightly browned on all sides. Remove from skillet.

3. Add shallots, garlic, jalapeño and ginger to skillet. Stir-fry 2 to 3 minutes. Add broccoli; stir-fry 1 minute. Cover and cook 3 minutes or until broccoli is crisp-tender.

4. Drain noodles; add to skillet and stir to combine. Return tofu to skillet; add soy sauces and fish sauce. Stir-fry about 8 minutes or until noodles are coated and flavors are blended. Adjust seasoning. Garnish with basil.

Szechuan Beef Lo Mein

Makes 4 servings

1 boneless beef top sirloin
  steak (about 1 pound)

4 cloves garlic, minced

2 teaspoons minced fresh
  ginger

¾ teaspoon red pepper flakes,
  divided

1 tablespoon vegetable oil

1 can (about 14 ounces)
  vegetable broth

1 cup water

2 tablespoons soy sauce

1 package (8 ounces) frozen
  mixed vegetables for
  stir-fry

1 package (9 ounces)
  refrigerated angel hair
  pasta*

¼ cup chopped fresh cilantro
  (optional)

*Or use dried pasta if fresh is not
available.*

1. Cut beef in half lengthwise, then crosswise into thin slices. Toss beef with garlic, ginger and ½ teaspoon red pepper flakes in large bowl.

2. Heat oil in large nonstick skillet over medium-high heat. Add half of beef to skillet; stir-fry 2 minutes or until meat is barely pink in center. Remove from skillet; set aside. Repeat with remaining beef.

3. Add broth, water, soy sauce and remaining ¼ teaspoon red pepper flakes to skillet; bring to a boil over high heat. Add vegetables; return to a boil. Reduce heat to low; cover and simmer 3 minutes or until vegetables are crisp-tender.

4. Uncover; stir in pasta. Return to a boil over high heat. Reduce heat to medium; simmer, uncovered, 2 minutes, separating pasta with two forks. Return beef and any accumulated juices to skillet; simmer 1 minute or until pasta is tender and beef is heated through. Sprinkle with cilantro, if desired.

Pad Thai

Makes 4 to 6 servings

8 ounces uncooked rice noodles, ⅛ inch wide

2 tablespoons rice wine vinegar

1½ tablespoons fish sauce

1 to 2 tablespoons fresh lemon juice

1 tablespoon ketchup

2 teaspoons sugar

¼ teaspoon red pepper flakes

1 tablespoon vegetable oil

1 boneless skinless chicken breast (about 4 ounces), finely chopped

2 green onions, thinly sliced

2 cloves garlic, minced

3 ounces small raw shrimp, peeled

2 cups fresh bean sprouts

¾ cup shredded red cabbage

1 medium carrot, shredded

3 tablespoons minced fresh cilantro

2 tablespoons chopped unsalted dry-roasted peanuts

Lime wedges

1. Place noodles in medium bowl. Cover with lukewarm water; let stand 30 minutes or until soft. Drain and set aside. Combine vinegar, fish sauce, lemon juice, ketchup, sugar and red pepper flakes in small bowl.

2. Heat oil in wok or large nonstick skillet over medium-high heat. Add chicken, green onions and garlic. Cook and stir until chicken is no longer pink. Stir in noodles; cook 1 minute. Add shrimp; cook about 3 minutes or just until shrimp turn pink and opaque. Stir in fish sauce mixture; toss to coat evenly. Add bean sprouts; cook 2 minutes or until heated through.

3. Serve with shredded cabbage, carrot, cilantro, peanuts and lime wedges.

Chicken Ramen Noodle Bowls

Makes 6 servings

1 tablespoon olive oil

1 pound boneless skinless chicken thighs

1 large yellow onion, peeled and halved

6 cups chicken broth

2 tablespoons soy sauce

4 green onions, divided

1 (1-inch) piece fresh ginger, sliced

1 clove garlic

6 ounces shiitake mushrooms, thinly sliced

⅓ cup hoisin sauce

8 ounces uncooked fresh Chinese noodles

3 hard-cooked eggs, cut in half lengthwise

¼ cup thinly sliced red bell pepper

Fresh cilantro leaves

SLOW COOKER DIRECTIONS

1. Heat oil in large skillet over medium-high heat. Add chicken; cook 8 to 10 minutes or until browned. Remove chicken to slow cooker using slotted spoon. Add onion halves to skillet, cut side down; cook 4 to 5 minutes or until lightly charred. Remove onion halves to slow cooker. Add broth, soy sauce, 2 green onions, ginger and garlic. Cover; cook on LOW 6 to 7 hours or on HIGH 3 to 4 hours or until chicken is tender.

2. Remove chicken to large cutting board; shred with two forks. Strain broth into large bowl. Discard solids; return broth to slow cooker. Stir in mushrooms and hoisin sauce. Cover; cook on HIGH 30 minutes.

3. Divide noodles and broth evenly among 6 bowls. Top each bowl evenly with chicken, mushrooms, one egg half, bell pepper and cilantro. Chop remaining 2 green onions; sprinkle evenly over bowls.

Spicy Sesame Noodles

Makes 6 servings

6 ounces uncooked soba (buckwheat) noodles

2 teaspoons dark sesame oil

1 tablespoon sesame seeds

½ cup vegetable broth

1 tablespoon creamy peanut butter

½ cup thinly sliced green onions

½ cup minced red bell pepper

4 teaspoons soy sauce

1½ teaspoons finely chopped seeded jalapeño pepper

1 clove garlic, minced

¼ teaspoon red pepper flakes

1. Cook noodles according to package directions. (Do not overcook.) Rinse under cold water until cool; drain well. Place noodles in large bowl; toss with oil.

2. Cook sesame seeds in small skillet over medium heat about 3 minutes or until seeds begin to pop and turn golden brown, stirring frequently. Remove from skillet.

3. Whisk broth and peanut butter in medium bowl until blended. (Mixture may look curdled.) Stir in green onions, bell pepper, soy sauce, jalapeño, garlic and red pepper flakes.

4. Pour mixture over noodles; toss to coat. Cover and let stand 30 minutes at room temperature or refrigerate up to 24 hours. Sprinkle with toasted sesame seeds before serving.

Cellophane Noodles with Minced Pork

Makes 4 servings

1   package (about 4 ounces) uncooked cellophane noodles*

32 dried shiitake mushrooms

2   tablespoons minced fresh ginger

2   tablespoons black bean sauce

1½ cups chicken broth

1   tablespoon dry sherry

1   tablespoon soy sauce

2   tablespoons vegetable oil

6   ounces lean ground pork

3   green onions, sliced

1   jalapeño or other hot pepper, seeded and finely chopped

Sliced red peppers (optional)

Cellophane noodles (also called bean threads or glass noodles) are thin, translucent noodles sold in tangled bunches.

1. Place noodles and dried mushrooms in separate bowls; cover each with hot water. Let stand 30 minutes; drain.

2. Cut noodles into 4-inch pieces. Squeeze out excess water from mushrooms. Cut off and discard stems; thinly slice caps.

3. Combine ginger and black bean sauce in small bowl. Combine broth, sherry and soy sauce in medium bowl.

4. Heat oil in wok or large skillet over high heat. Add pork; stir-fry 2 minutes or until no longer pink. Add green onions, jalapeño and black bean sauce mixture; stir-fry 1 minute.

5. Add broth mixture, noodles and mushrooms. Simmer, uncovered, about 5 minutes or until most of liquid is absorbed. Garnish with red peppers.

Sesame Noodle Cake

Makes 4 servings

4 ounces uncooked vermicelli or Chinese egg noodles

1 tablespoon soy sauce

1 tablespoon peanut or vegetable oil

½ teaspoon dark sesame oil

1. Cook noodles according to package directions; drain well. Place in large bowl. Toss with soy sauce until sauce is absorbed.

2. Heat 10- or 11-inch nonstick skillet over medium heat. Add peanut oil; heat until hot. Add noodle mixture; pat into even layer with spatula.

3. Cook, uncovered, 6 minutes or until bottom is lightly browned. Invert onto plate, then slide back into skillet, browned side up. Cook 4 minutes or until bottom is well browned. Drizzle with sesame oil. Transfer to cutting board; cut into quarters.

Peanutty Thai Pasta

Makes 4 servings

8   ounces uncooked spaghetti

½   cup half-and-half

¼   cup creamy peanut butter

1   tablespoon honey

2   teaspoons soy sauce

1   teaspoon lemon juice

1   teaspoon minced fresh
      ginger

⅛   teaspoon red pepper flakes

1   cup shredded carrots

¼   cup sliced green onions

      Chopped peanuts and
      chopped fresh cilantro

1. Cook pasta according to package directions. Drain and return to saucepan; keep warm.

2. Combine half-and-half, peanut butter, honey, soy sauce, lemon juice, ginger and red pepper flakes in medium saucepan. Cook and stir over medium heat 4 minutes or until smooth and creamy; pour over pasta.

3. Add carrots and green onions; mix well. Sprinkle with peanuts and cilantro.

Sukiyaki

Makes 4 servings

1 package (about 4 ounces) uncooked cellophane noodles*

½ cup beef broth

½ cup teriyaki sauce

¼ cup sake, rice wine or dry sherry

1 tablespoon sugar

1 pound beef tenderloin or top sirloin steaks

2 tablespoons vegetable oil, divided

6 ounces fresh shiitake mushrooms, stems removed and sliced

8 ounces firm tofu, drained and cut into 1-inch cubes

6 green onions, cut into 2-inch pieces

8 ounces fresh spinach, stems removed

Cellophane noodles (also called bean threads or glass noodles) are thin, translucent noodles sold in tangled bunches.

1. Place noodles in bowl; cover with hot water. Let stand 30 minutes or until softened; drain. Cut into 4-inch lengths; set aside.

2. Combine broth, teriyaki sauce, sake and sugar in small bowl; mix well. Set aside. Cut beef crosswise into ¼-inch strips.

3. Heat wok over high heat 1 minute. Drizzle 1 tablespoon oil into wok and heat 30 seconds. Add half of beef; stir-fry 3 minutes or until browned. Remove to bowl; set aside. Repeat with remaining 1 tablespoon oil and beef.

4. Reduce heat to medium. Add mushrooms to wok; stir-fry 1 minute and move to one side of wok. Add tofu to bottom of wok; cook 1 minute, stirring gently. Move to another side of wok. Add green onions to bottom of wok. Add broth mixture and bring to a boil. Move onions up side of wok.

5. Add noodles and spinach, keeping each in separate piles and stirring gently to soften in teriyaki sauce. Push up side of wok. Add beef and any juices; heat through.

Bean Threads with Tofu and Vegetables

Makes 6 servings

8   ounces firm tofu, drained
    and cubed

1   tablespoon dark sesame oil

3   teaspoons soy sauce, divided

1   can (about 14 ounces)
    vegetable broth

1   package (about 4 ounces)
    uncooked cellophane
    noodles*

1   package (16 ounces) frozen
    mixed vegetable medley
    such as broccoli, carrots
    and water chestnuts,
    thawed

¼   cup rice wine vinegar

½   teaspoon red pepper flakes

*Cellophane noodles (also called
bean threads or glass noodles) are
thin, translucent noodles sold in
tangled bunches.*

1. Place tofu on shallow plate; drizzle with oil and 1½ teaspoons soy sauce.

2. Combine broth and remaining 1½ teaspoons soy sauce in deep skillet or large saucepan. Bring to a boil over high heat; reduce heat. Add noodles; simmer, uncovered, 7 minutes or until liquid is absorbed, stirring occasionally to separate noodles.

3. Stir in vegetables and vinegar; heat through. Stir in tofu mixture and red pepper flakes; heat through.

Vegetarian Rice Noodles

Makes 4 servings

½ cup soy sauce

⅓ cup sugar

¼ cup lime juice

2 fresh red Thai chiles *or* 1 large jalapeño pepper, finely chopped

8 ounces uncooked thin rice noodles (rice vermicelli)

¼ cup vegetable oil

8 ounces firm tofu, drained and cut into triangles

1 jicama (8 ounces), peeled and chopped *or* 1 can (8 ounces) sliced water chestnuts, drained

2 medium sweet potatoes (1 pound), peeled and cut into ¼-inch-thick slices

2 large leeks, cut into ¼-inch-thick slices

¼ cup chopped unsalted dry-roasted peanuts

2 tablespoons chopped fresh mint

2 tablespoons chopped fresh cilantro

1. Combine soy sauce, sugar, lime juice and chiles in small bowl until well blended; set aside.

2. Place noodles in medium bowl. Cover with hot water; let stand 15 minutes or until soft. Drain well; cut into 3-inch lengths.

3. Meanwhile, heat oil in large skillet over medium-high heat. Add tofu; stir-fry 4 minutes per side or until golden brown. Remove with slotted spatula to paper towel-lined baking sheet.

4. Add jicama to skillet; stir-fry 5 minutes or until lightly browned. Remove to baking sheet. Stir-fry sweet potatoes in batches until tender and browned; remove to baking sheet. Add leeks; stir-fry 1 minute; remove to baking sheet.

5. Stir soy sauce mixture; add to skillet. Heat until sugar dissolves. Add noodles; toss to coat. Gently stir in tofu, vegetables, peanuts, mint and cilantro.

Vegetable Beef Noodle Soup

Makes 6 servings

1 tablespoon vegetable oil

8 ounces beef for stew, cut into ½-inch pieces

¾ cup unpeeled cubed potato (1 medium)

½ cup sliced carrot

1 tablespoon balsamic vinegar

¾ teaspoon dried thyme

½ teaspoon salt

¼ teaspoon black pepper

2½ cups beef broth

1 cup water

¼ cup chili sauce or ketchup

2 ounces uncooked thin egg noodles

¾ cup jarred or canned pearl onions, rinsed and drained

¼ cup frozen peas

1. Heat oil in large saucepan over medium-high heat. Add beef; cook 3 minutes or until browned on all sides, stirring occasionally. Remove to plate.

2. Add potato, carrot, vinegar, thyme, salt and pepper to saucepan; cook and stir over medium heat 3 minutes. Add broth, water and chili sauce. Bring to a boil over medium-high heat; add beef. Reduce heat to medium-low; cover and simmer 30 minutes or until meat is almost fork-tender.

3. Return to a boil over medium-high heat. Add noodles; cover and cook 7 to 10 minutes or until noodles are tender, stirring occasionally. Add onions and peas; cook 1 minute or until heated through. Serve immediately.

Szechuan Cold Noodles

Makes 4 servings

8 ounces uncooked vermicelli, broken in half, or Chinese egg noodles

3 tablespoons rice vinegar

3 tablespoons soy sauce

2 tablespoons peanut or vegetable oil

1 clove garlic, minced

1 teaspoon minced fresh ginger

1 teaspoon dark sesame oil

½ teaspoon crushed Szechuan peppercorns or red pepper flakes

½ cup coarsely chopped fresh cilantro

¼ cup chopped peanuts

1. Cook noodles according to package directions; drain.

2. Combine vinegar, soy sauce, peanut oil, garlic, ginger, sesame oil and peppercorns in large bowl. Add noodles; toss to coat. Sprinkle with cilantro and peanuts. Serve at room temperature or chilled.

SZECHUAN VEGETABLE NOODLES: Add 1 cup chopped peeled cucumber, ½ cup *each* chopped red bell pepper, cucumber and sliced green onions and an additional 1 tablespoon soy sauce.

ITALIAN NOODLES

Venetian Chicken with Creamy Pesto Sauce

Makes 4 servings

1 tablespoon olive oil

1 red or yellow bell pepper, cut into chunks

1 pound boneless skinless chicken breasts or thighs, cut into 1-inch chunks

½ teaspoon salt

¼ teaspoon black pepper

½ cup prepared pesto sauce

½ cup half-and-half

3 cups hot cooked spaghetti or vermicelli pasta (6 ounces uncooked)

¼ cup grated Asiago or Parmesan cheese

1. Heat oil in large nonstick skillet over medium heat. Add bell pepper; cook and stir 3 minutes. Add chicken, salt and pepper; cook and stir 5 minutes.

2. Stir in pesto and half-and-half; cook, stirring occasionally, 3 minutes or until chicken is cooked through and bell pepper is tender (about 5 minutes for chicken thighs).

3. Serve over pasta; sprinkle with cheese.

Spaghetti and Beets Aglio e Olio

Makes 6 servings

2 medium beets, peeled

8 ounces uncooked spaghetti or thin spaghetti

⅓ cup plus 2 tablespoons olive oil, divided

1 cup fresh Italian or French bread crumbs*

4 cloves garlic, very thinly sliced

¾ teaspoon salt

½ teaspoon red pepper flakes

½ cup chopped fresh Italian parsley

¾ cup shredded Parmesan cheese, divided

*To make fresh bread crumbs, tear 2 ounces bread into pieces; process in food processor until coarse crumbs form.

1. Spiral beets with fine ribbon blade of spiralizer; cut into desired lengths. Cook spaghetti according to package directions. Drain and return to saucepan, reserving ½ cup water; keep warm. Meanwhile, heat 1 tablespoon oil in large nonstick skillet over medium-high heat. Add beets; cook and stir 8 to 10 minutes or until tender.

2. Heat 1 tablespoon oil in large skillet over medium heat. Add bread crumbs; cook 4 to 5 minutes or until golden brown, stirring frequently. Transfer to small bowl.

3. Add remaining ⅓ cup oil, garlic, salt and red pepper flakes to same skillet; cook about 3 minutes or until garlic just begins to brown on edges.

4. Add pasta, beets and parsley to skillet; toss to coat with oil mixture. Add some of reserved pasta water to moisten pasta, if desired. Stir in bread crumbs and ½ cup cheese. Top with remaining ¼ cup cheese just before serving.

Cavatappi with Sausage Meatballs

Makes 4 servings

8 ounces uncooked cavatappi or rigatoni pasta

8 ounces bulk mild Italian sausage

8 ounces ground beef

1 onion, chopped

1 can (about 14 ounces) diced tomatoes

1 can (6 ounces) tomato paste

½ teaspoon dried oregano

¼ teaspoon salt

⅓ cup grated Parmesan cheese

1. Cook pasta according to package directions. Drain; set aside.

2. Shape sausage into small marble-size meatballs. Brown meatballs in large skillet over medium-high heat 3 minutes, stirring frequently. Remove from skillet. Add beef and onion to same skillet; cook until beef is no longer pink, stirring to break up meat. Drain fat.

3. Stir in meatballs, tomatoes, tomato paste, oregano and salt. Simmer 10 minutes. Stir in pasta. Sprinkle with cheese.

Classic Fettuccine Alfredo

Makes 4 servings

12   ounces uncooked dried or
      fresh fettuccine

⅔   cup whipping cream

6   tablespoons (¾ stick) butter

½   teaspoon salt

      Generous dash white pepper

      Generous dash ground
      nutmeg

1   cup grated Parmesan cheese

2   tablespoons chopped fresh
      Italian parsley

1. Cook pasta according to package directions. Drain well. Return to saucepan; cover and keep warm.

2. Meanwhile, heat cream and butter in large heavy skillet over medium-low heat until butter melts and mixture bubbles, stirring frequently. Cook and stir 2 minutes. Stir in salt, pepper and nutmeg. Remove from heat; gradually stir in Parmesan until well blended and smooth. Return to low heat, if necessary; do not let sauce bubble or cheese will become lumpy and tough.

3. Pour sauce over pasta. Cook and stir over low heat 2 to 3 minutes or until sauce is thickened and pasta is evenly coated. Sprinkle with parsley. Serve immediately.

Puttanesca with Angel Hair Pasta

Makes 4 to 6 servings

2 tablespoons olive oil

2 to 3 anchovy fillets, chopped

3 cloves garlic, minced

2 tablespoons tomato paste

2 cans (15 ounces each) diced tomatoes

1 teaspoon dried oregano

1 teaspoon dried basil

½ teaspoon salt

¼ teaspoon black pepper

1 can (14 ounces) tomato sauce

½ cup pitted Greek olives, coarsely chopped

2 tablespoons rinsed and drained capers

½ to 1½ teaspoons red pepper flakes

12 ounces uncooked fresh or dried angel hair pasta

1. Heat oil in skillet over medium-low heat. Add anchovies; cook and stir 2 to 3 minutes. Add garlic; cook until lightly browned. Add tomato paste; cook 2 minutes.

2. Stir in tomatoes, oregano, basil, salt and black pepper. Increase heat to medium; cook about 30 minutes or until tomatoes break down and mixture becomes saucy, stirring occasionally. Meanwhile, bring large saucepan of water to a boil.

3. Reduce heat to medium-low. Add tomato sauce, olives capers and red pepper flakes; simmer 10 minutes.

4. Cook pasta according to package directions. Drain; toss with sauce.

Spaghetti Aglio e Olio

Makes 4 servings

8 ounces uncooked spaghetti or thin spaghetti

⅓ cup plus 1 tablespoon olive oil, divided

1 cup fresh Italian or French bread crumbs*

4 cloves garlic, very thinly sliced

¾ teaspoon salt

½ teaspoon red pepper flakes

½ cup chopped fresh Italian parsley

¾ cup shredded Parmesan cheese, divided

To make fresh bread crumbs, tear 2 ounces bread into pieces; process in food processor until coarse crumbs form.

1. Cook pasta according to package directions. Drain, reserving ½ cup cooking water, and return to saucepan; keep warm.

2. Meanwhile, heat 1 tablespoon oil in large skillet over medium heat. Add bread crumbs; cook 4 to 5 minutes or until golden brown, stirring frequently. Transfer to small bowl; set aside.

3. Add remaining ⅓ cup oil, garlic, salt and red pepper flakes to same skillet; cook about 3 minutes or until garlic just begins to brown on edges.

4. Add pasta and parsley to skillet; toss to coat. Add some of reserved pasta water to moisten pasta, if desired. Stir in bread crumbs and ½ cup cheese. Top with remaining ¼ cup cheese before serving.

Classic Lasagna

Makes 6 to 8 servings

1 tablespoon olive oil

8 ounces bulk mild Italian sausage

8 ounces ground beef

1 medium onion, chopped

3 cloves garlic, minced, divided

1½ teaspoons salt, divided

1 can (28 ounces) crushed tomatoes

1 can (28 ounces) diced tomatoes

2 teaspoons Italian seasoning

1 egg

1 container (15 ounces) ricotta cheese

¾ cup grated Parmesan cheese, divided

½ cup minced fresh parsley

¼ teaspoon black pepper

12 uncooked no-boil lasagna noodles

4 cups (16 ounces) shredded mozzarella

1. Preheat oven to 350°F. Spray 13×9-inch baking dish with nonstick cooking spray.

2. Heat oil in large saucepan over medium-high heat. Add sausage, beef, onion, 2 cloves garlic and 1 teaspoon salt; cook and stir 10 minutes or until meat is no longer pink, breaking up meat with wooden spoon. Add tomatoes and Italian seasoning; bring to a boil. Reduce heat to medium low; cook 15 minutes, stirring occasionally.

3. Meanwhile, beat egg in medium bowl. Stir in ricotta cheese, ½ cup Parmesan cheese, parsley, remaining 1 clove garlic, ½ teaspoon salt and black pepper until well blended.

4. Spread ¼ cup sauce in prepared baking dish. Top with 3 noodles, breaking to fit if necessary. Spread one third of ricotta mixture over noodles. Sprinkle with 1 cup mozzarella cheese; top with 2 cups sauce. Repeat layers of noodles, ricotta mixture, mozzarella cheese and sauce two times. Top with remaining 3 noodles, remaining sauce, remaining 1 cup mozzarella cheese and ¼ cup Parmesan cheese. Cover with foil sprayed with nonstick cooking spray.

5. Bake 40 to 45 minutes or until hot and bubbly, removing foil after 30 minutes. Let stand 10 minutes before serving.

Creamy Fettuccine with Prosciutto and Peas

Makes 2 servings

8   ounces uncooked fettuccine

2   tablespoons olive oil

4   cloves garlic, minced

3   ounces thinly sliced
    prosciutto or salami, cut
    into thin strips

1   cup peas

1   cup half-and-half or
    whipping cream

½   teaspoon salt

½   teaspoon black pepper

1   cup freshly grated Parmesan
    cheese

1. Cook pasta according to package directions; drain.

2. Meanwhile, heat oil in large skillet over medium heat. Add garlic; cook and stir 2 minutes. Add prosciutto and peas; cook and stir 2 minutes. Stir in half-and-half, salt and pepper; cook and stir 3 minutes.

3. Add pasta to skillet; stir to coat with sauce. Stir in cheese. Serve immediately.

Italian Three-Cheese Macaroni

Makes 4 servings

2 cups uncooked elbow macaroni

¼ cup (½ stick) butter

3 tablespoons all-purpose flour

1 teaspoon Italian seasoning

½ teaspoon salt

½ teaspoon black pepper

2 cups milk

¾ cup (3 ounces) shredded Cheddar cheese

¼ cup grated Parmesan cheese

1 can (about 14 ounces) diced tomatoes, drained

1 cup (4 ounces) shredded mozzarella cheese

½ cup dry bread crumbs

1. Preheat oven to 350°F. Spray 2-quart casserole with nonstick cooking spray.

2. Cook pasta according to package directions until al dente. Drain and set aside.

3. Melt butter in medium saucepan over medium heat. Whisk in flour, Italian seasoning, salt and pepper, stirring until smooth. Gradually whisk in milk in thin steady stream. Cook until slightly thickened, whisking constantly. Add Cheddar and Parmesan cheeses; stir until smooth.

4. Layer half of pasta, half of tomatoes and half of cheese sauce in prepared dish. Repeat layers.

5. Sprinkle mozzarella cheese and bread crumbs evenly over casserole.

6. Bake, covered, 30 minutes or until heated through. Uncover and bake 5 minutes or until top is golden brown.

Spaghetti alla Bolognese

Makes 4 to 6 servings

2 tablespoons olive oil

1 pound ground beef

1 medium onion, chopped

½ small carrot, finely chopped

½ stalk celery, finely chopped

1 cup dry white wine

½ cup milk

⅛ teaspoon ground nutmeg

1 can (about 14 ounces) whole peeled tomatoes, coarsely chopped, juice reserved

1 cup beef broth

3 tablespoons tomato paste

1 teaspoon salt

1 teaspoon dried basil

½ teaspoon dried thyme

⅛ teaspoon black pepper

1 bay leaf

1 pound uncooked spaghetti

1 cup freshly grated Parmesan cheese

1. Heat oil in large saucepan over medium heat. Add beef; cook 6 to 8 minutes, stirring to break up meat. Drain fat.

2. Add onion, carrot and celery; cook and stir 2 minutes. Stir in wine; cook 4 to 6 minutes or until wine has evaporated. Stir in milk and nutmeg; cook 3 to 4 minutes or until milk has almost evaporated. Remove from heat.

3. Press tomatoes with reserved juice through sieve into meat mixture; discard seeds.

4. Stir in broth, tomato paste, salt, basil, thyme, pepper and bay leaf; bring to a boil over medium-high heat. Reduce heat; simmer 1 to 1½ hours or until most of liquid has evaporated and sauce thickens, stirring frequently. Remove and discard bay leaf.

5. Cook spaghetti according to package directions; drain. Combine spaghetti and meat sauce in large bowl; toss gently to coat. Sprinkle with cheese.

Orecchiette with Sausage and Broccoli Rabe

Makes 4 to 6 servings

1 tablespoon olive oil

1 pound mild Italian sausage

2 cloves garlic, minced

⅛ teaspoon red pepper flakes

1½ pounds broccoli rabe, stems trimmed, cut into 2-inch pieces

1 package (16 ounces) uncooked orecchiette

¾ cup grated Parmesan cheese

Salt and black pepper

1. Bring large pot of salted water to a boil.

2. Meanwhile, heat oil in large skillet over medium-high heat. Remove sausage from casings; add to skillet. Cook sausage about 8 minutes or until browned, stirring to break up meat. Drain fat. Add garlic and red pepper flakes; cook and stir 3 minutes.

3. Add broccoli rabe to boiling water; cook 2 minutes. Remove broccoli rabe with slotted spoon; transfer to skillet with sausage mixture. Cook over medium-low heat until crisp-tender, stirring occasionally.

4. Add pasta to boiling water; cook according to package directions. Drain pasta, reserving 1 cup cooking water. Combine pasta, sausage mixture and Parmesan in large serving bowl; mix well. Season with salt and black pepper to taste. Add some of reserved cooking water if sauce is dry. Serve immediately with additional Parmesan, if desired.

Stuffed Shells

Makes 8 servings

1 package (12 ounces) uncooked jumbo pasta shells

2 tablespoons olive oil

3 cloves garlic, halved

12 ounces ground veal

12 ounces ground pork

1 package (10 ounces) frozen chopped spinach, thawed and squeezed dry

1 cup fresh parsley, finely chopped

1 cup dry bread crumbs

2 eggs, beaten

3 tablespoons grated Parmesan cheese

3 cloves garlic, minced

Salt

3 cups pasta sauce

1. Preheat oven to 375°F. Grease 12×8-inch baking pan.

2. Cook shells according to package directions; drain.

3. Heat oil in large skillet over medium heat. Add halved garlic cloves; cook and stir until lightly browned. Discard garlic. Add veal and pork; cook until browned, stirring to break up meat. Drain fat. Cool slightly.

4. Combine spinach, parsley, bread crumbs, eggs, cheese and minced garlic in large bowl; blend well. Season with salt. Add meat; blend well. Fill shells with mixture. Spread about 1 cup pasta sauce in bottom of prepared pan. Arrange shells in pan. Pour remaining pasta sauce over shells.

5. Bake, covered, 35 to 45 minutes or until hot and bubbly.

Classic Pesto with Linguine

Makes 4 servings

12 ounces uncooked linguine

2 tablespoons butter

¼ cup plus 1 tablespoon olive oil, divided

2 tablespoons pine nuts

1 cup tightly packed fresh basil leaves

2 cloves garlic

¼ teaspoon salt

¼ cup grated Parmesan cheese

1½ tablespoons grated Romano cheese

1. Cook pasta according to package directions; drain. Toss with butter in large serving bowl; set aside and keep warm.

2. Meanwhile, heat 1 tablespoon oil in small skillet over medium-low heat. Add pine nuts; cook and stir 30 to 45 seconds until light brown, shaking pan constantly. Remove with slotted spoon; drain on paper towels.

3. Place toasted pine nuts, basil, garlic and salt in food processor or blender. With processor running, add remaining ¼ cup oil in slow steady stream; process until evenly blended and pine nuts are finely chopped.

4. Transfer basil mixture to small bowl. Stir in Parmesan and Romano cheeses.

5. Add pesto sauce to pasta; toss until well coated. Serve immediately.

Fettuccine with Vegetable Marinara Sauce

Makes 4 to 6 servings

2 tablespoons extra virgin olive oil

1 medium onion, finely chopped

1 small carrot, finely chopped

1 small stalk celery, finely chopped

2 cloves garlic, finely chopped

1 can (28 ounces) peeled plum tomatoes, undrained

½ cup water

⅓ cup packed chopped fresh basil leaves

Salt and freshly ground black pepper

1 package (12 to 16 ounces) uncooked fresh fettuccine

2 tablespoons butter, thinly sliced

Freshly grated Parmesan cheese

1. Heat oil in large saucepan over medium heat. Add onion, carrot, celery and garlic. Cover and cook about 5 minutes or until onion is golden and tender, stirring occasionally.

2. Drain tomatoes, reserving juice. Coarsely crush tomatoes with fingers or wooden spoon. Add tomatoes, reserved juice and water to saucepan; bring to a boil over high heat. Reduce heat to medium-low. Simmer, uncovered, about 45 minutes or until slightly thickened and reduced, stirring frequently. Stir in basil during last 5 minutes of cooking. Season to taste with salt and pepper.

3. Meanwhile, cook pasta according to package directions until barely tender. Drain and return to saucepan. Add butter; toss gently until pasta is coated and butter melts. Serve sauce over pasta; top with Parmesan cheese.

Fettuccine alla Carbonara

Makes 4 servings

12 ounces uncooked fettuccine

4 ounces pancetta or bacon, cut crosswise into ½-inch pieces

3 cloves garlic, cut into halves

¼ cup dry white wine

⅓ cup whipping cream

1 egg

1 egg yolk

⅔ cup grated Parmesan cheese, divided

Dash white pepper

1. Cook pasta according to package directions. Drain and return to saucepan; keep warm.

2. Cook and stir pancetta and garlic in large skillet over medium-low heat 4 minutes or until lightly browned. Drain and discard all but 2 tablespoons drippings from skillet.

3. Add wine to skillet; cook over medium heat 3 minutes or until wine is almost evaporated. Add cream; cook and stir 2 minutes. Remove from heat; discard garlic.

4. Whisk egg and egg yolk in top of double boiler; place over simmering water, adjusting heat to maintain simmer. Whisk ⅓ cup cheese and pepper into egg mixture; cook and stir until thickened.

5. Pour pancetta mixture over fettuccine; toss to coat. Cook over medium-low heat until heated through. Add egg mixture; toss to coat. Serve with remaining ⅓ cup cheese.

Pasta and Potatoes with Pesto

Makes 6 servings

3 medium red potatoes, cut into chunks

8 ounces uncooked linguine

¾ cup frozen peas

1 package (about 7 ounces) prepared pesto sauce

¼ cup plus 2 tablespoons grated Parmesan cheese, divided

¼ teaspoon salt

¼ teaspoon black pepper

1. Place potatoes in medium saucepan; cover with water. Bring to a boil over high heat; reduce heat. Cook, uncovered, 10 minutes or until potatoes are tender; drain.

2. Meanwhile, cook linguine according to package directions, adding peas during last 3 minutes of cooking; drain. Return pasta mixture to pan; add potatoes, pesto sauce, ¼ cup cheese, salt and pepper, tossing until blended.

3. Sprinkle with remaining 2 tablespoons cheese.

Eggplant Rigatoni

Makes 4 to 6 servings

8 ounces uncooked whole wheat rigatoni

2 tablespoons olive oil, divided

2 medium eggplants, peeled and cut into 1-inch cubes

½ cup (2 ounces) herb goat cheese

Salt and black pepper

1. Cook pasta according to package directions. Reserve 1 cup of cooking water; drain.

2. Heat 1 tablespoon oil in large nonstick skillet over medium heat. Add eggplant; cook and stir 20 minutes or until eggplant is soft and golden brown.

3. Add reserved cooking water to eggplant; stir well. Add pasta, goat cheese, remaining 1 tablespoon oil, salt and pepper. Toss to combine; cook until heated through.

MEDITERRANEAN NOODLES

Lentil and Orzo Pasta Salad

Makes 4 servings

8 cups water

1½ teaspoons salt, divided

½ cup dried lentils, rinsed and sorted

4 ounces uncooked orzo

1½ cups quartered grape tomatoes

¾ cup finely chopped celery

½ cup chopped red onion

2 ounces pitted olives (about 16 olives), coarsely chopped

¼ cup cider vinegar

1 tablespoon olive oil

1 tablespoon dried basil

1 clove garlic, minced

⅛ teaspoon red pepper flakes

4 ounces feta cheese with sun-dried tomatoes and basil

1. Bring water and 1 teaspoon salt to boil in Dutch oven over high heat. Add lentils; boil 12 minutes.

2. Add orzo; cook 10 minutes or just until tender. Drain. Rinse under cold water until cool; drain well.

3. Meanwhile, combine tomatoes, celery, onion, olives, vinegar, oil, basil, garlic, remaining ½ teaspoon salt and red pepper flakes in large bowl; set aside.

4. Add lentil mixture to tomato mixture; toss gently to blend. Add cheese; toss gently. Let stand 15 minutes before serving.

Greek Chicken and Pasta

Makes 4 servings

6   ounces uncooked fettuccine
    or whole wheat fettuccine

1   jar (6 ounces) marinated
    artichoke hearts

1   tablespoon olive oil

1   small red bell pepper, cut
    into very thin strips

3   cloves garlic, minced

1   pound boneless skinless
    chicken breasts, cut into
    bite-size pieces

1   tablespoon plus 1 teaspoon
    lemon juice

2   teaspoons dried oregano

1   teaspoon grated lemon peel

¼   to ½ teaspoon dried mint
    (optional)

¼   teaspoon black pepper

⅓   cup sliced pitted black olives

¼   cup crumbled feta cheese

1. Cook pasta according to package directions. Drain and return to saucepan; cover to keep warm.

2. Drain artichoke hearts, reserving marinade. Cut artichoke hearts into quarters; set aside.

3. Heat oil in large skillet. Add bell pepper and garlic; cook and stir over medium heat until tender. Remove from skillet.

4. Add chicken to skillet; cook and stir 2 to 3 minutes or until chicken is nearly cooked through.

5. Return bell pepper mixture to skillet. Add reserved artichoke marinade, lemon juice, oregano, lemon peel, mint, if desired, and black pepper to skillet; bring to a boil. Reduce heat; simmer, uncovered, 1 to 2 minutes or until chicken is no longer pink. Stir in artichoke hearts and olives. Toss with hot cooked pasta. Sprinkle with feta cheese.

Lemon Salmon and Spinach Pasta

Makes 4 servings

12 ounces salmon fillet

8 ounces uncooked fettuccine

1 tablespoon butter

1 teaspoon finely grated lemon peel

½ teaspoon salt

¼ teaspoon red pepper flakes

2 cloves garlic, minced

2 tablespoons lemon juice

3 cups baby spinach leaves

½ cup shredded carrot

1. Pat salmon dry with paper towels. Remove skin from salmon; discard. Cut fish into ½-inch pieces.

2. Cook pasta according to package directions. Drain and return to saucepan.

3. Meanwhile, melt butter in large skillet over medium-high heat. Add salmon, lemon peel, salt, red pepper flakes and garlic; cook about 5 minutes or until salmon flakes when tested with fork. Gently stir in lemon juice.

4. Add salmon mixture, spinach and carrot to hot cooked pasta; gently toss to combine. Serve immediately.

Fresh Vegetable Lasagna

Makes 8 servings

8 ounces uncooked lasagna noodles

1 package (10 ounces) frozen chopped spinach, thawed and squeezed dry

1 cup shredded carrots

½ cup sliced green onions

½ cup sliced red bell pepper (1-inch pieces)

¼ cup chopped fresh parsley

1 teaspoon salt, divided

½ teaspoon black pepper

1 package (15 ounces) ricotta cheese

½ cup buttermilk

2 eggs

1 cup sliced mushrooms

1 can (14 ounces) artichoke hearts, rinsed, drained and chopped

2 cups (8 ounces) shredded mozzarella cheese

¼ cup grated Parmesan cheese

1. Cook pasta according to package directions; drain. Rinse under cold water until cool; drain well. Set aside.

2. Preheat oven to 375°F. Combine spinach, carrots, green onions, bell pepper, parsley, ½ teaspoon salt and black pepper in large bowl; set aside.

3. Combine ricotta cheese, buttermilk, eggs and remaining ½ teaspoon salt in food processor or blender. Cover; process until smooth.

4. Spray 13×9-inch baking pan with nonstick cooking spray. Arrange one third of lasagna noodles in bottom of pan. Spread with half of cheese mixture, half of vegetable mixture, half of mushrooms, half of artichokes and ¾ cup mozzarella cheese. Repeat layers, ending with noodles. Sprinkle with remaining ½ cup mozzarella and Parmesan cheeses.

5. Cover; bake 30 minutes. Remove cover; continue baking 20 minutes or until bubbly and heated through. Let stand 10 minutes before cutting.

Lemon-Mint Meatballs with Lemon Orzo

Makes 4 servings

6   cloves garlic, divided

12 ounces ground chicken

2   green onions, minced

2   tablespoons minced fresh
    mint

1   egg

3   teaspoons grated lemon
    peel, divided

1   teaspoon salt, divided

½   teaspoon dried oregano

¼   teaspoon black pepper

3   cups chicken broth

1   cup (6 ounces) uncooked
    orzo pasta

1   tablespoon lemon juice

1   package (about 5 ounces)
    fresh spinach leaves, torn

1. Spray 11×7-inch microwavable baking dish with nonstick cooking spray.

2. Mince 3 cloves garlic. Combine chicken, green onions, mint, egg, 2 teaspoons lemon peel, minced garlic, ½ teaspoon salt, oregano and pepper in medium bowl; mix until well blended. Shape into 12 meatballs and place in baking dish, spacing evenly apart.

3. Slice remaining 3 cloves garlic; place in large saucepan. Add broth and remaining ½ teaspoon salt; bring to a boil over high heat. Stir in orzo. Reduce heat to medium; simmer 8 to 10 minutes or until tender. Reduce heat to low; stir in remaining 1 teaspoon lemon peel and lemon juice. Stir in spinach, one handful at a time, until incorporated. Stir until spinach is wilted. Remove from heat; cover to keep warm.

4. Place meatballs in microwave. Microwave on HIGH 2 minutes. Rearrange meatballs, moving them from outer edges to center of dish. Microwave on HIGH 1 to 2 minutes until cooked through (160°F).

5. Spoon orzo into wide bowls or rimmed plates. Top with meatballs.

Tomato, Brie and Noodle Casserole

Makes 6 servings

1 pint grape tomatoes, halved

2 teaspoons olive oil

¾ teaspoon salt, divided

2 tablespoons butter

1 clove garlic, smashed

2 tablespoons all-purpose flour

2 cups half-and-half, heated

8 ounces good-quality ripe Brie, rind removed, cut into small chunks

¼ cup finely chopped fresh basil

2 tablespoons minced fresh chives

¼ teaspoon pepper

6 ounces egg noodles, cooked (about 3½ to 4 cups uncooked)

¼ cup sliced almonds

1. Preheat oven to 425°F. Line large baking sheet with heavy-duty foil. Spray 9-inch square baking dish with nonstick cooking spray.

2. Spread tomatoes on prepared baking sheet; drizzle with oil and sprinkle with ¼ teaspoon salt. Roast 20 minutes or until tomatoes are tender and slightly shriveled. Set aside. *Reduce oven temperature to 350°F.*

3. Melt butter in large saucepan or deep skillet over medium heat. Add garlic clove and cook 1 minute. Stir in flour until blended. Gradually add half-and-half; cook and stir until thickened. Remove and discard garlic. Gradually stir in cheese until melted.

4. Add basil, chives, remaining ½ teaspoon salt and pepper. Stir in noodles. Drain off any liquid from tomatoes; fold into noodle mixture. Spread in prepared baking dish.

5. Bake 17 to 20 minutes or until sauce starts to bubble. Sprinkle with almonds; bake 8 to 10 minutes or until nuts are light golden brown.

Baked Chicken and Garlic Orzo

Makes 4 servings

1 tablespoon plus 2 teaspoons olive oil, divided

4 chicken breast halves, skinned

¼ cup dry white wine

10 ounces uncooked orzo pasta

1 cup chopped onions

4 cloves garlic, minced

2 tablespoons chopped fresh parsley

1 teaspoon dried oregano

1 can (about 14 ounces) chicken broth

¼ cup water

Paprika

1 teaspoon lemon-pepper seasoning

½ teaspoon salt

1 lemon, cut into 8 wedges

1. Preheat oven to 350°F. Heat 1 tablespoon oil in large nonstick skillet over medium-high heat. Add chicken; cook 1 to 2 minutes per side or until lightly browned. Remove chicken from skillet; set aside.

2. Reduce heat to medium-high; add wine. Stir with flat spatula, scraping brown bits from bottom of skillet. Cook 30 seconds or until slightly reduced; set aside.

3. Spray 9-inch square baking pan with nonstick cooking spray. Add orzo, onions, garlic, parsley, oregano, broth, water and wine mixture; stir. Place chicken breasts on top. Sprinkle lightly with paprika and lemon-pepper seasoning.

4. Bake, uncovered, 1 hour 10 minutes. Remove chicken. Add salt and remaining 2 teaspoons oil to baking pan; mix well. Place chicken on top. Serve with fresh lemon wedges.

Koshari

Makes 6 to 8 servings

4 cups water

1 cup uncooked white basmati rice, rinsed and drained

1 cup uncooked brown lentils, rinsed and sorted

3 teaspoons kosher salt, divided

1 teaspoon ground cinnamon, divided

¼ teaspoon ground nutmeg, divided

1 cup uncooked elbow macaroni

¼ cup olive oil

1 large onion, thinly sliced

1 large onion, diced

1 tablespoon minced garlic

1 teaspoon ground cumin

½ teaspoon ground coriander

¼ teaspoon red pepper flakes

¼ teaspoon black pepper

1 can (28 ounces) crushed tomatoes

2 teaspoons red wine vinegar

SLOW COOKER DIRECTIONS

1. Place water, rice, lentils, 2 teaspoons salt, ½ teaspoon cinnamon and ¼ teaspoon nutmeg in slow cooker. Cover; cook on HIGH 2 hours 30 minutes. Stir in macaroni. Cover; cook 30 minutes, stirring halfway through cooking time.

2. Meanwhile, heat oil in large skillet over medium-high heat. Add sliced onion; cook 12 minutes or until edges are dark brown and onion is softened. Transfer onion to medium bowl with slotted spoon. Season with ¼ teaspoon salt. Set aside.

3. Heat same skillet with oil over medium heat. Add diced onion; cook 8 minutes or until softened. Add garlic, cumin, coriander, remaining ½ teaspoon cinnamon, red pepper flakes, black pepper and remaining ¼ teaspoon nutmeg; cook 30 seconds or until fragrant. Stir in tomatoes, vinegar and remaining ¾ teaspoon salt; cook 8 to 10 minutes or until thickened, stirring occasionally.

4. Fluff rice mixture lightly before scooping into individual bowls. Top each serving evenly with tomato sauce and reserved onions.

Mediterranean Orzo and Vegetable Pilaf

Makes 6 servings

4 ounces (½ cup plus 2 tablespoons) uncooked orzo pasta

2 teaspoons olive oil

1 small onion, diced

2 cloves garlic, minced

1 small zucchini, diced

½ cup chicken broth

1 can (about 14 ounces) artichoke hearts, drained and quartered

1 medium tomato, chopped

½ teaspoon dried oregano

½ teaspoon salt

¼ teaspoon black pepper

½ cup crumbled feta cheese

Sliced black olives (optional)

1. Cook orzo according to package directions. Drain.

2. Heat oil in large nonstick skillet over medium heat. Add onion; cook and stir 5 minutes or until translucent. Add garlic; cook and stir 1 minute. Reduce heat to low. Add zucchini and broth; simmer 5 minutes or until zucchini is crisp-tender.

3. Add cooked orzo, artichokes, tomato, oregano, salt and pepper; cook and stir 1 minute or until heated through. Top with cheese and olives, if desired.

Salmon, Fettuccine and Cabbage

Makes 4 servings

1 package (9 ounces) uncooked fresh fettuccine

¼ cup plus 2 tablespoons seasoned rice vinegar

2 tablespoons vegetable oil

½ small head of cabbage, shredded (about 7 cups)

½ teaspoon whole fennel seeds

1 can (about 15 ounces) salmon, drained, flaked and bones removed

Salt and black pepper

1. Cook pasta according to package directions; drain.

2. Heat vinegar and oil in large skillet over medium-high heat. Add cabbage; cook 3 minutes or until crisp-tender, stirring occasionally.

3. Stir in fennel seeds. Add fettuccine; toss lightly to coat. Add salmon; mix lightly.

4. Heat thoroughly, stirring occasionally. Season with salt and pepper to taste.

METRIC CONVERSION CHART

VOLUME MEASUREMENTS (dry)

1/8 teaspoon = 0.5 mL
1/4 teaspoon = 1 mL
1/2 teaspoon = 2 mL
3/4 teaspoon = 4 mL
1 teaspoon = 5 mL
1 tablespoon = 15 mL
2 tablespoons = 30 mL
1/4 cup = 60 mL
1/3 cup = 75 mL
1/2 cup = 125 mL
2/3 cup = 150 mL
3/4 cup = 175 mL
1 cup = 250 mL
2 cups = 1 pint = 500 mL
3 cups = 750 mL
4 cups = 1 quart = 1 L

VOLUME MEASUREMENTS (fluid)

1 fluid ounce (2 tablespoons) = 30 mL
4 fluid ounces (1/2 cup) = 125 mL
8 fluid ounces (1 cup) = 250 mL
12 fluid ounces (1 1/2 cups) = 375 mL
16 fluid ounces (2 cups) = 500 mL

WEIGHTS (mass)

1/2 ounce = 15 g
1 ounce = 30 g
3 ounces = 90 g
4 ounces = 120 g
8 ounces = 225 g
10 ounces = 285 g
12 ounces = 360 g
16 ounces = 1 pound = 450 g

DIMENSIONS

1/16 inch = 2 mm
1/8 inch = 3 mm
1/4 inch = 6 mm
1/2 inch = 1.5 cm
3/4 inch = 2 cm
1 inch = 2.5 cm

OVEN TEMPERATURES

250°F = 120°C
275°F = 140°C
300°F = 150°C
325°F = 160°C
350°F = 180°C
375°F = 190°C
400°F = 200°C
425°F = 220°C
450°F = 230°C

BAKING PAN SIZES

Utensil	Size in Inches/Quarts	Metric Volume	Size in Centimeters
Baking or Cake Pan (square or rectangular)	8×8×2	2 L	20×20×5
	9×9×2	2.5 L	23×23×5
	12×8×2	3 L	30×20×5
	13×9×2	3.5 L	33×23×5
Loaf Pan	8×4×3	1.5 L	20×10×7
	9×5×3	2 L	23×13×7
Round Layer Cake Pan	8×1½	1.2 L	20×4
	9×1½	1.5 L	23×4
Pie Plate	8×1¼	750 mL	20×3
	9×1¼	1 L	23×3
Baking Dish or Casserole	1 quart	1 L	—
	1½ quart	1.5 L	—
	2 quart	2 L	—